Copyright © 2012 Mike Hoffman
All rights reserved.
ISBN: 149442052X
ISBN-13: 978-1494420529

Mike Hoffman

INTUITIVE ART

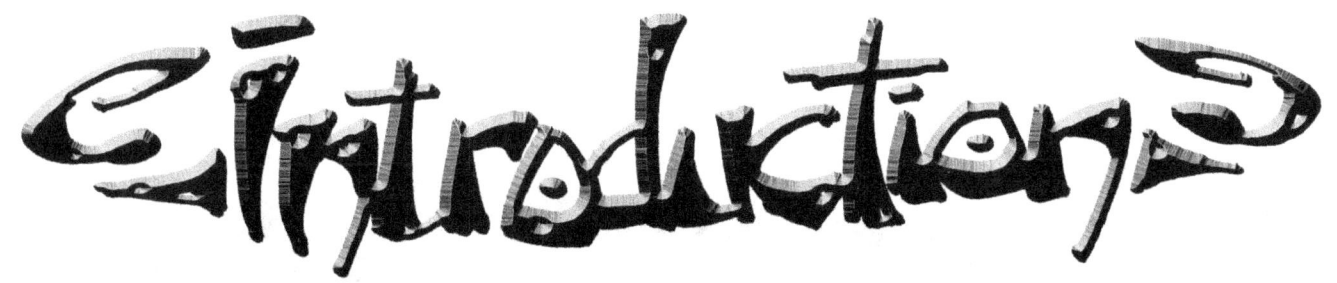

Introduction

The images in the book were created as part of a new artistic direction embarked on in early 2012. They are also much like examples presented in a related instructional book on "intuitive drawing".

After years of watching my pees and qyooz, and my earlobes, toenails and other pesky details so relevant to the mores of realistic illustration, I decided to stop all that nonsense and basically go solely on intuition.

But what's intuition, exactly, you ask; briefly, it is what pops into one's head before there is any chance to think. Yes, thinking can get you into trouble. Serious, deep trouble. In fact, it's what's wrong with the world today.

I found that the quietness that grew out of drawings that were never "right or wrong" was meditative. In a world of noise and constant distraction, much of it self-inflicted, this simple, primal act of making crude cavemanlike-marks began to send me to another place, essentially, from distraction towards clarity.

I realized that the path of ego and intellect was what created duality in the world, the good-versus-evil and us-vs-them systems that are omnipresent. I discovered also that only clarity provides an exit from egoic pursuits, and that after clarity is established then and only then can true "being" begin.

But don't take my word for it, you can experience all that for yourself.

On your marks...

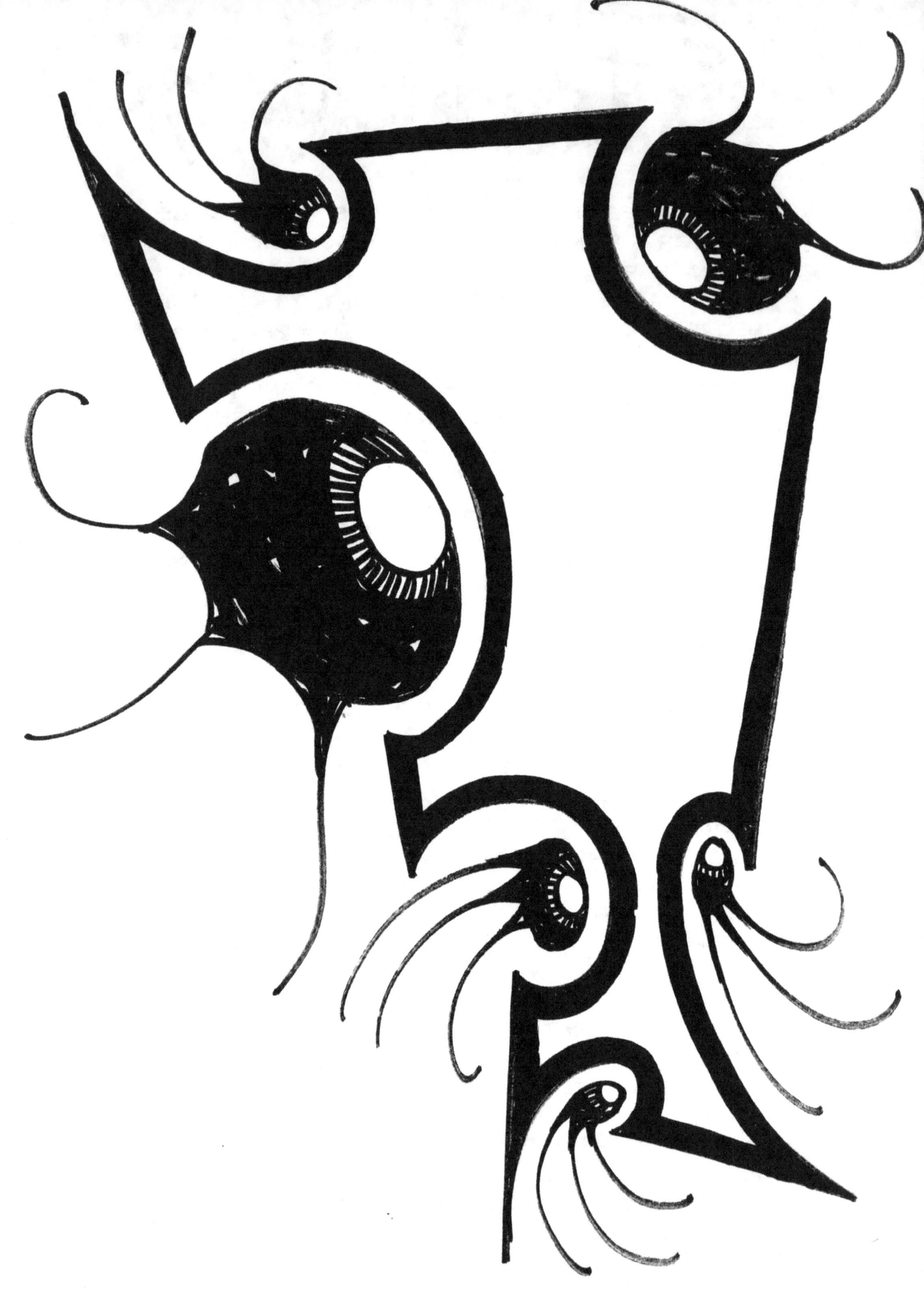

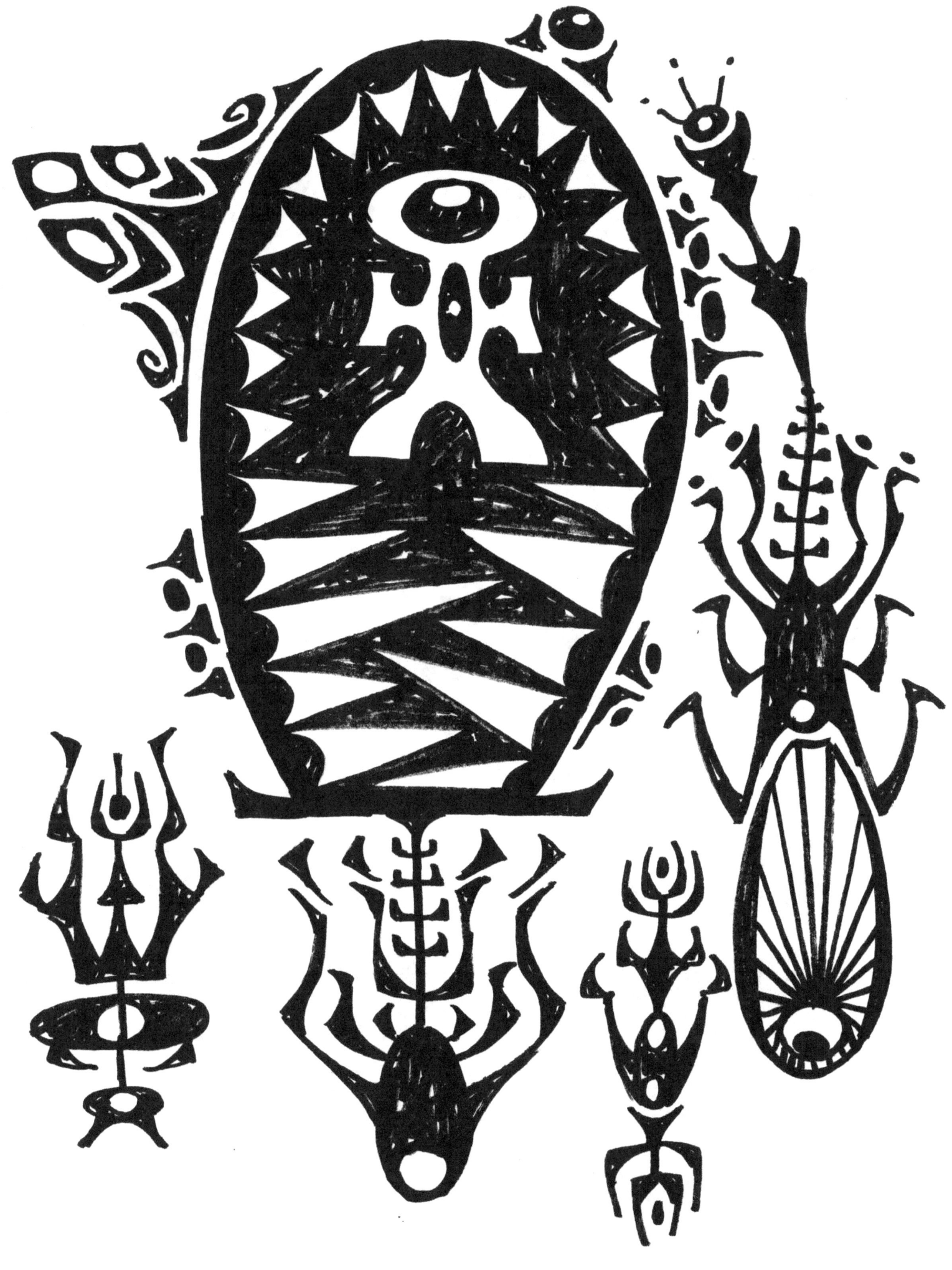

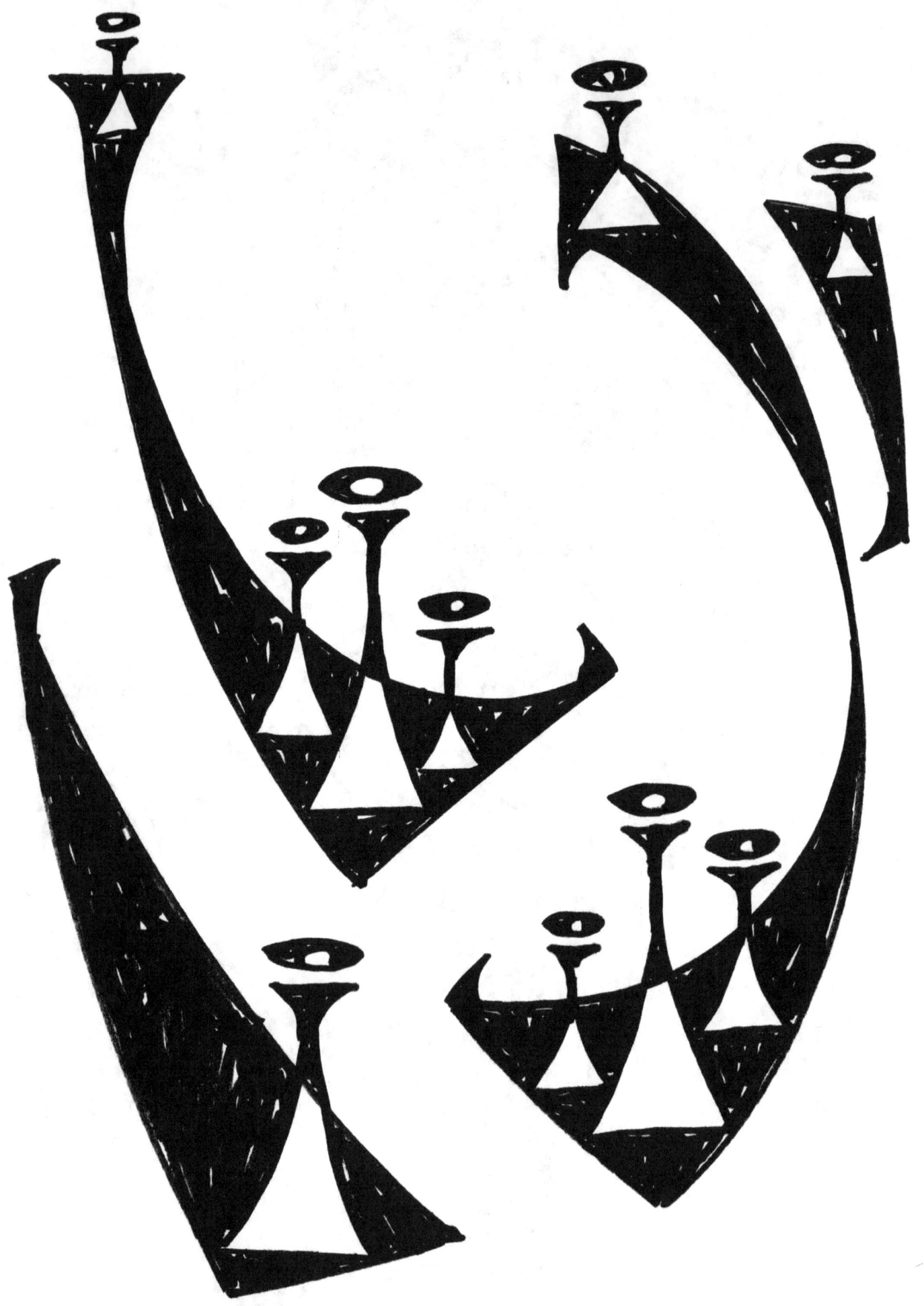

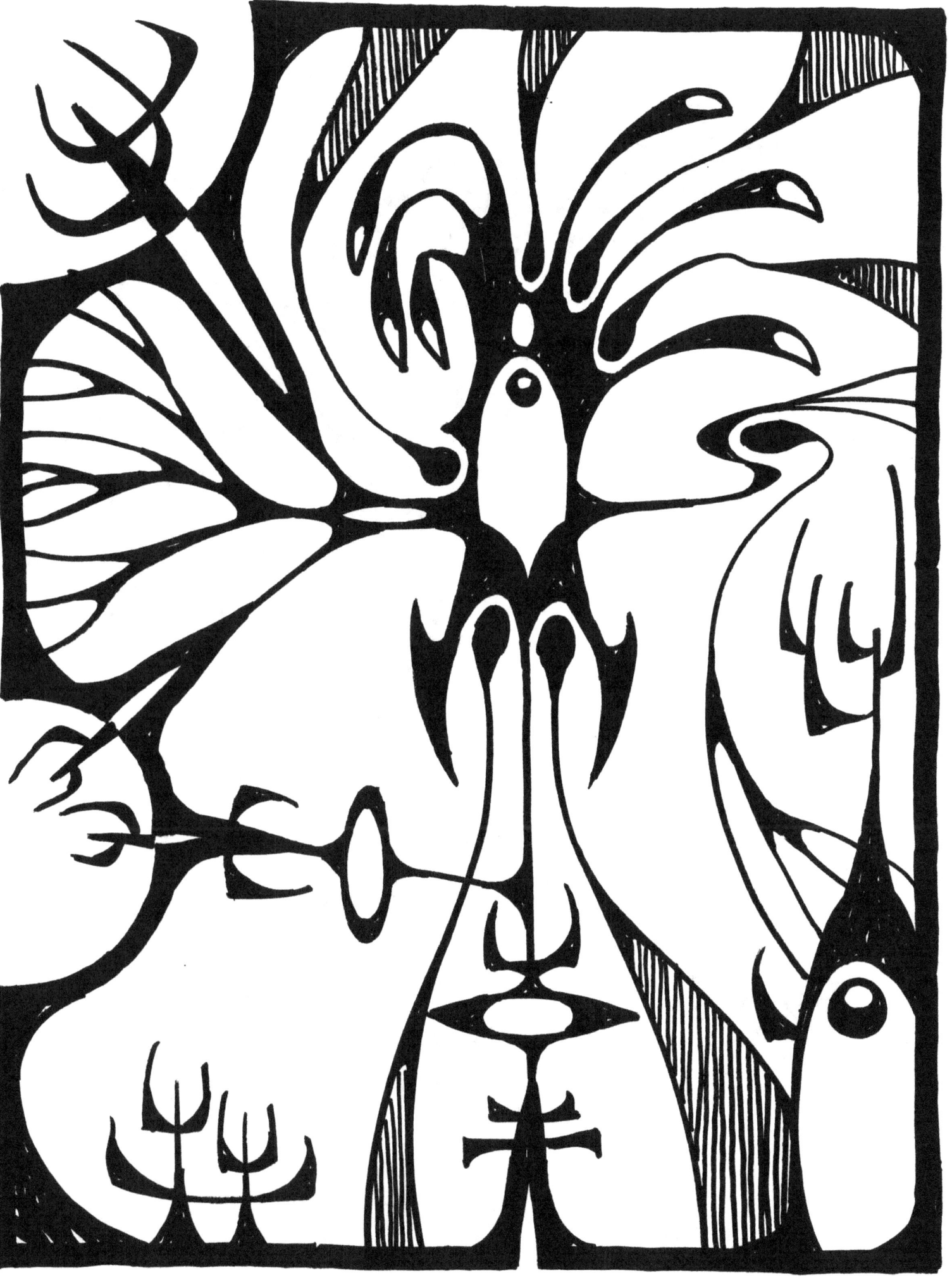

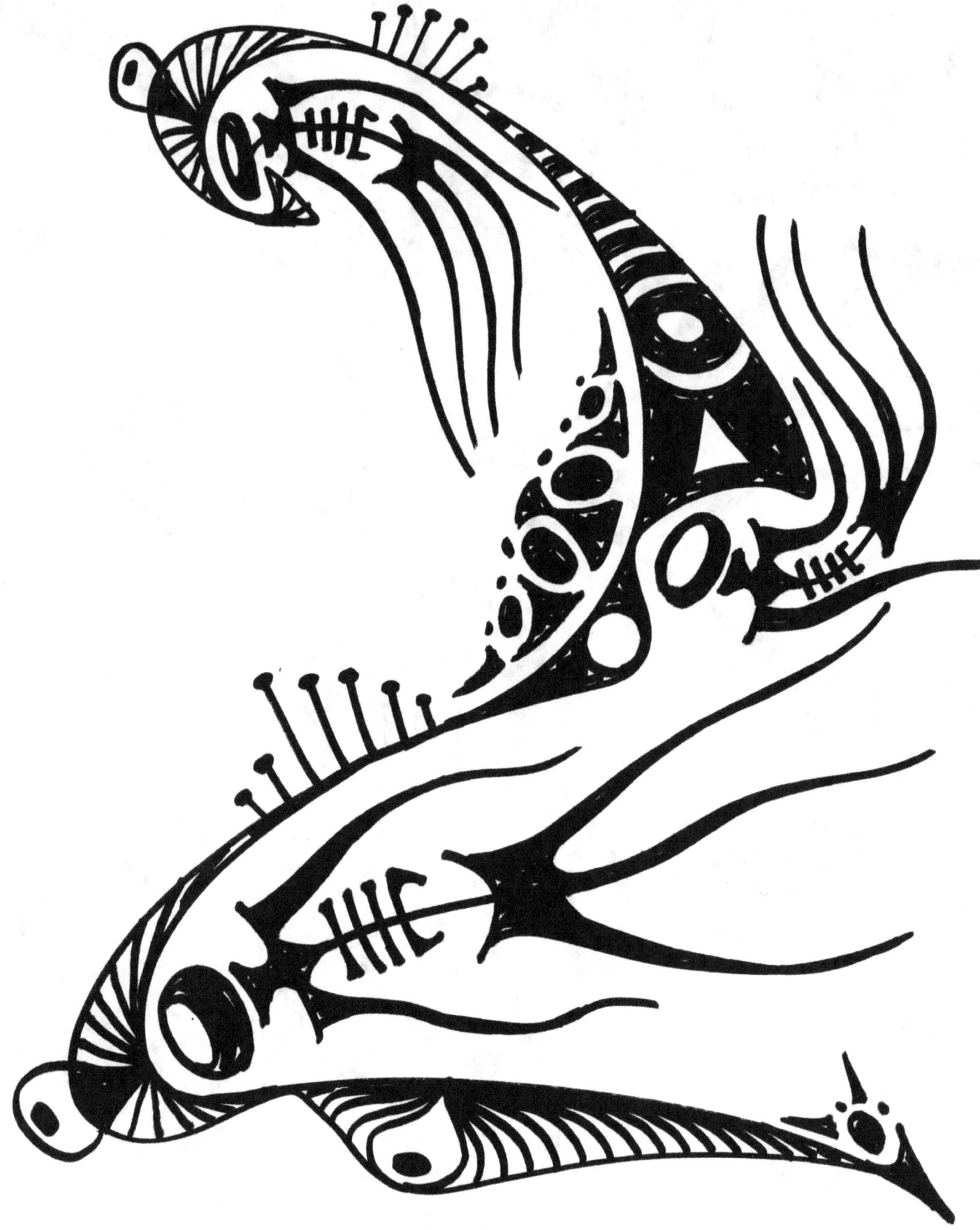

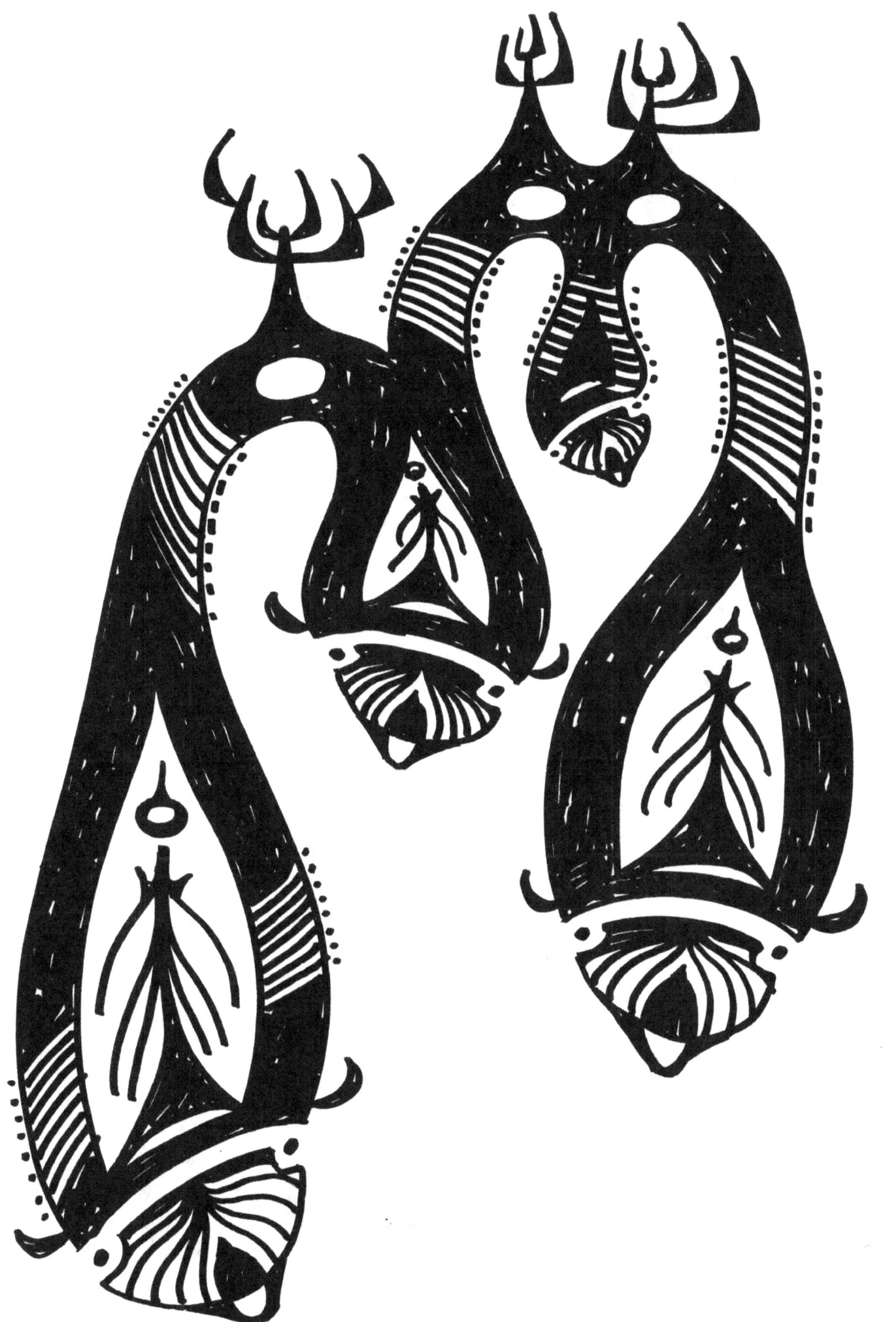

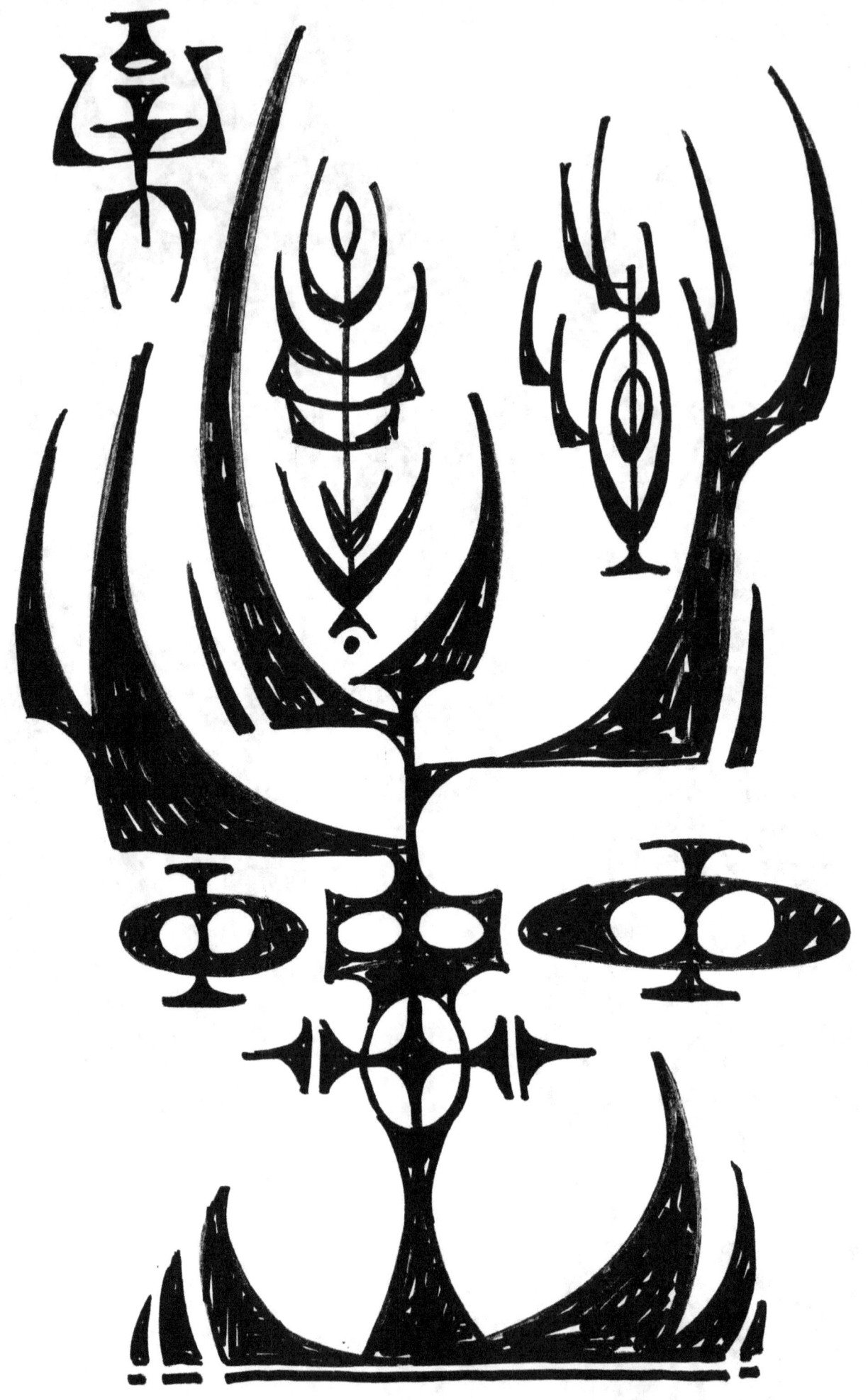

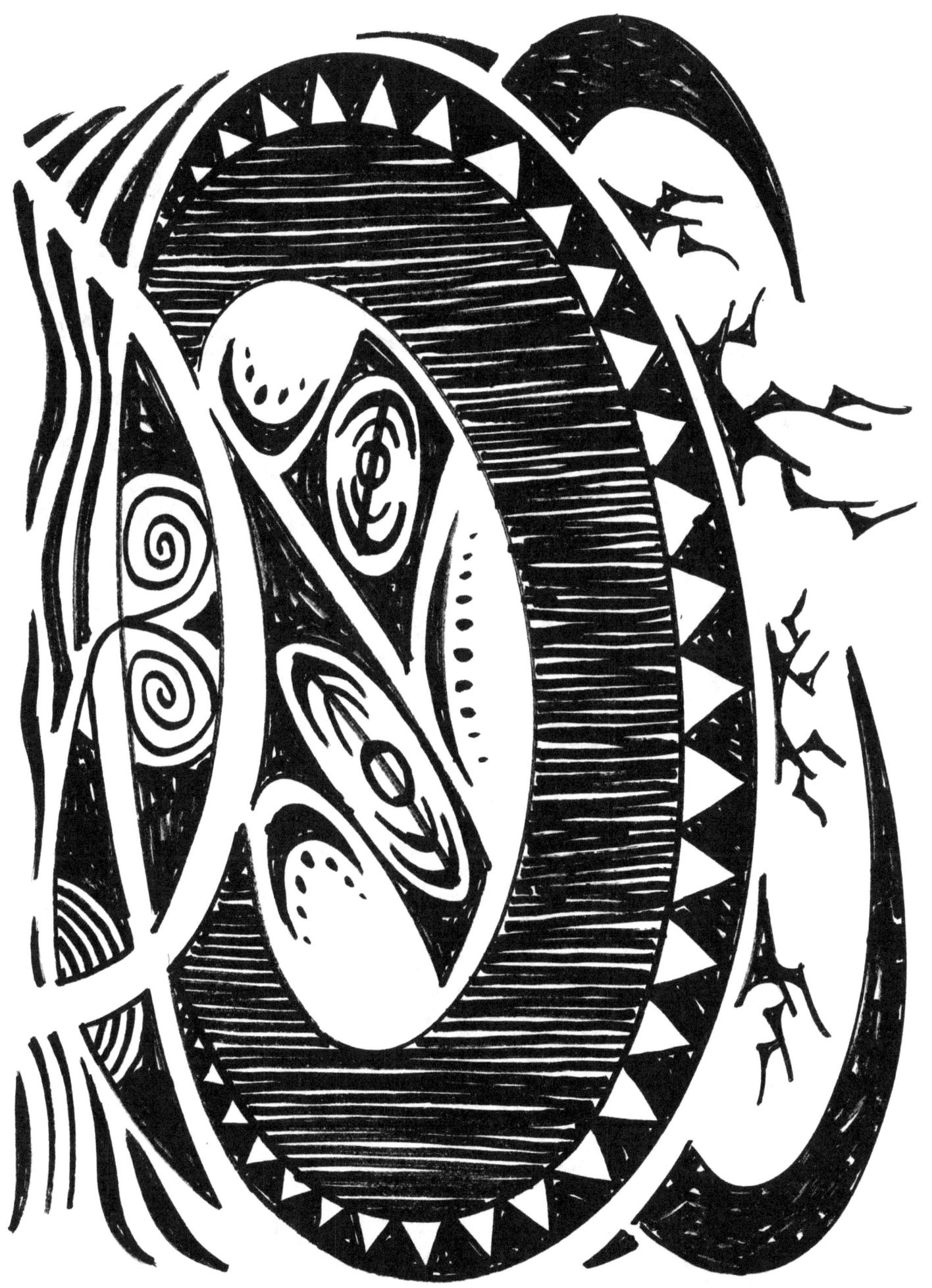

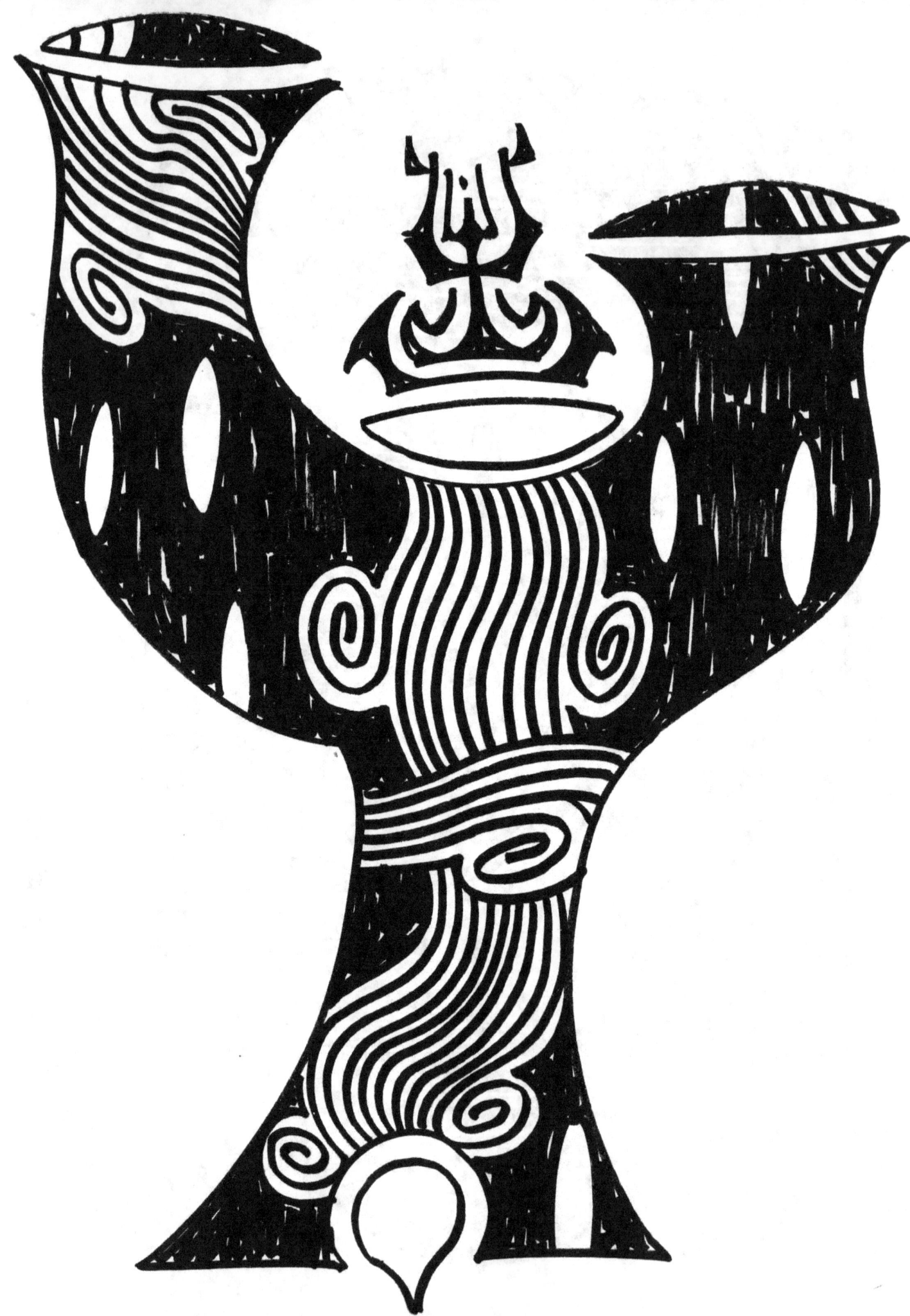

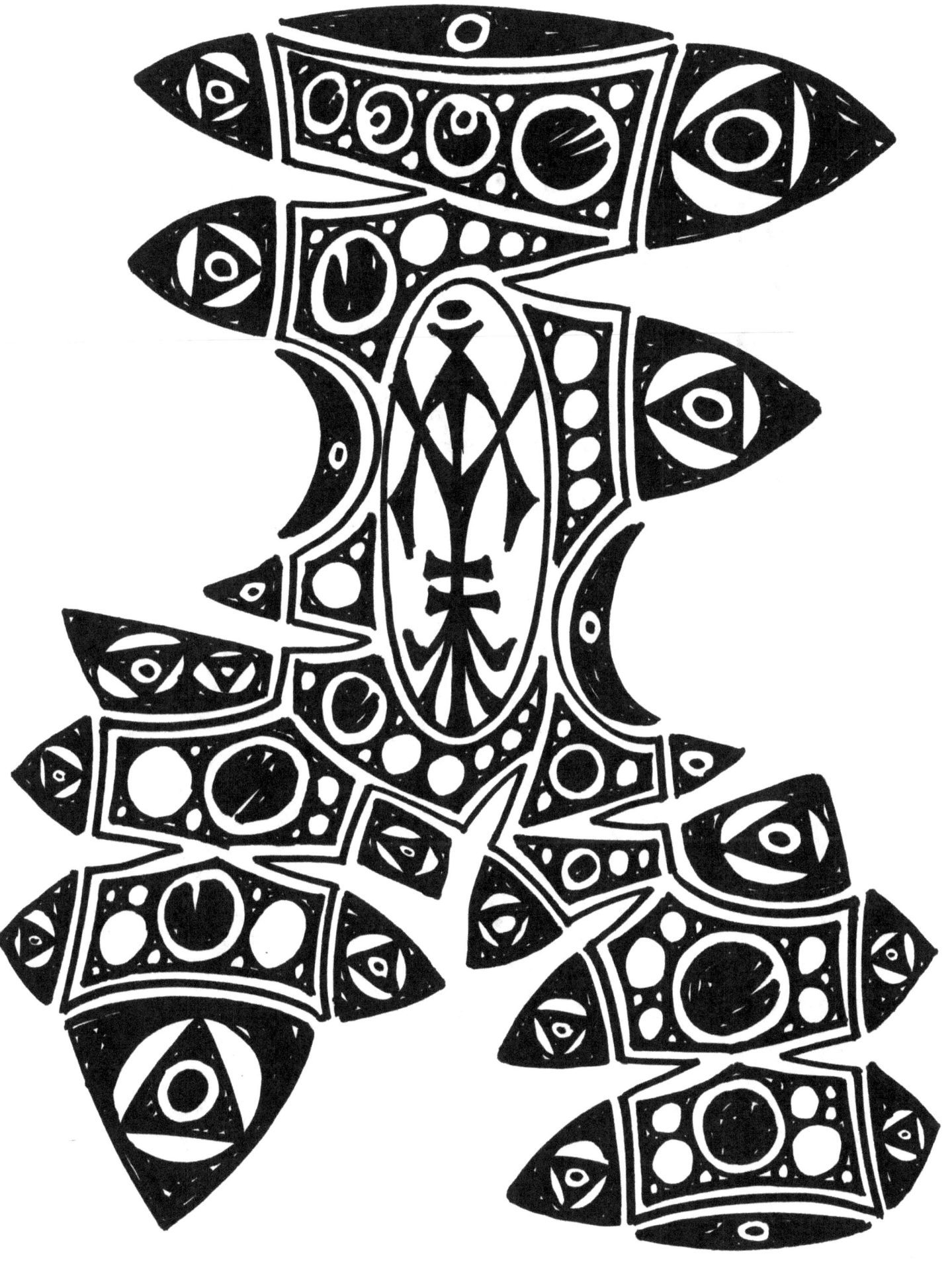

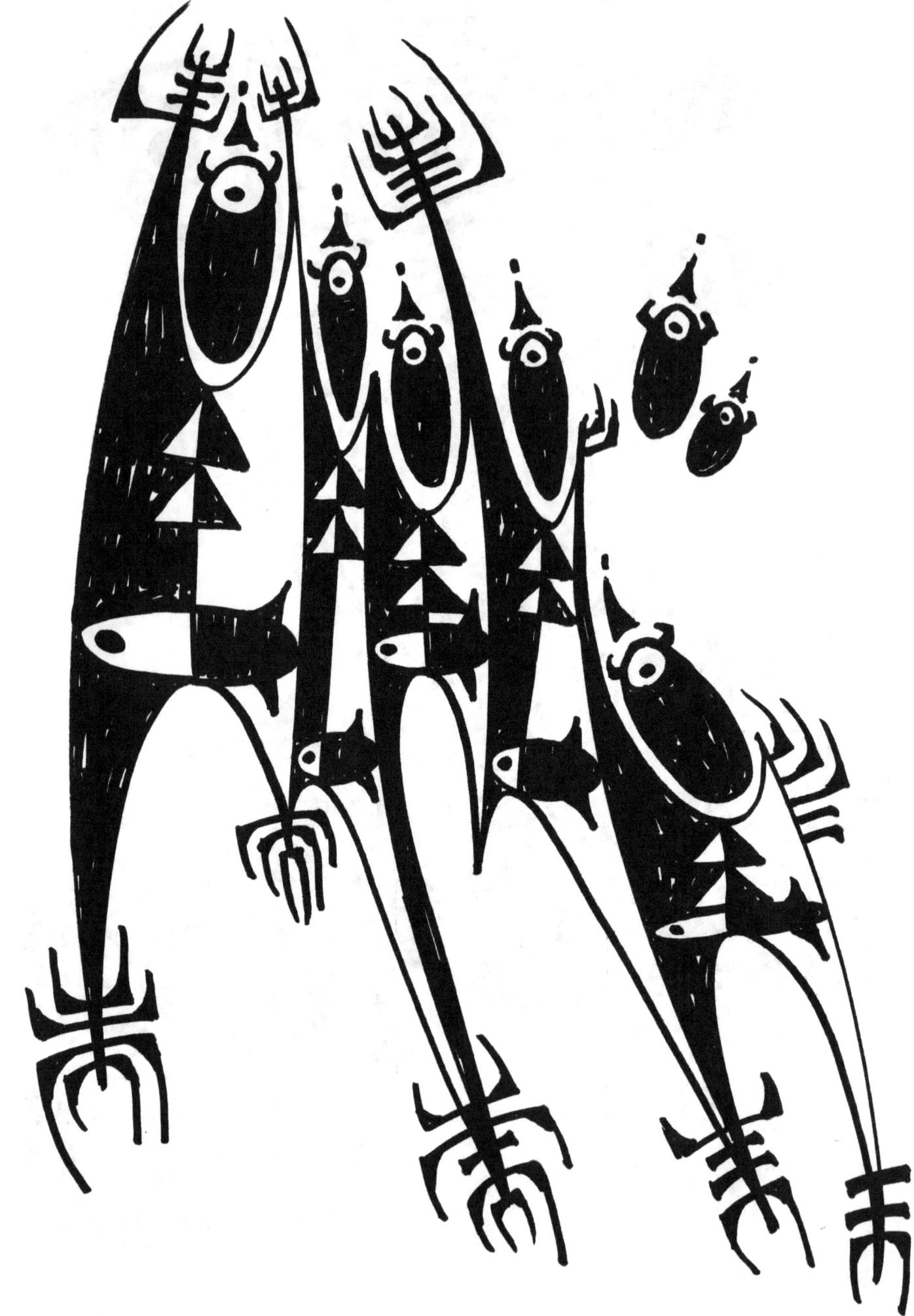

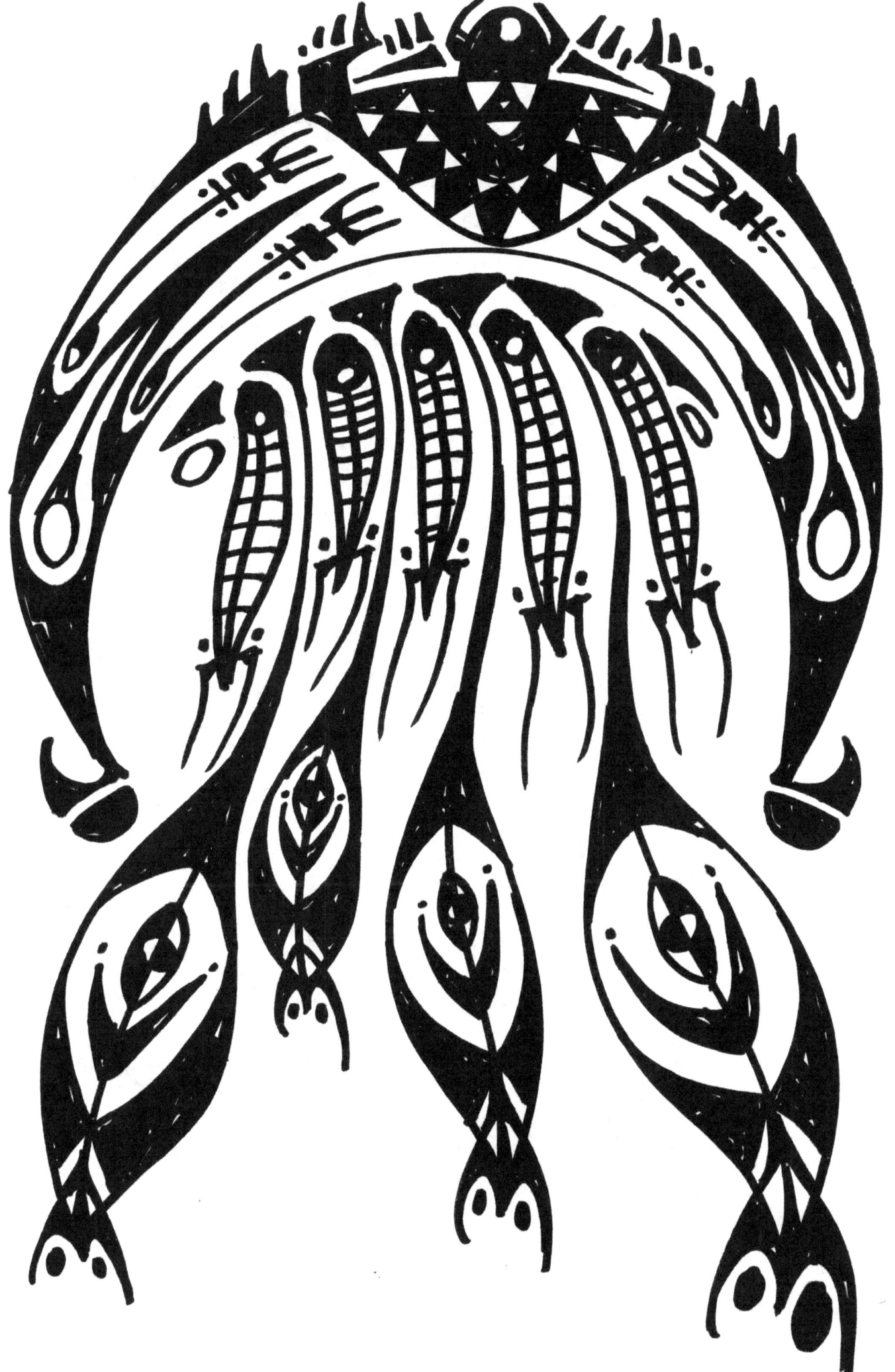

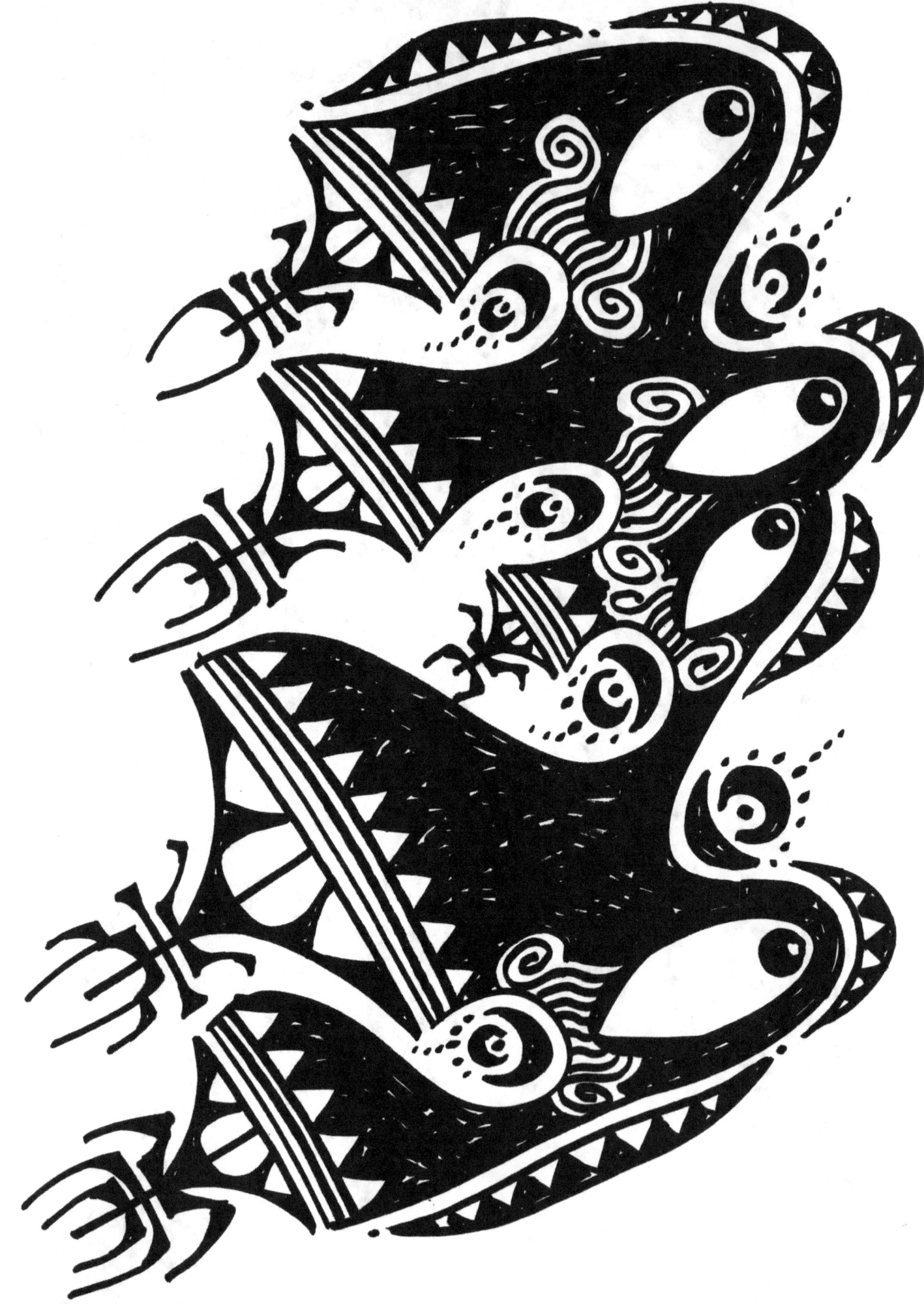

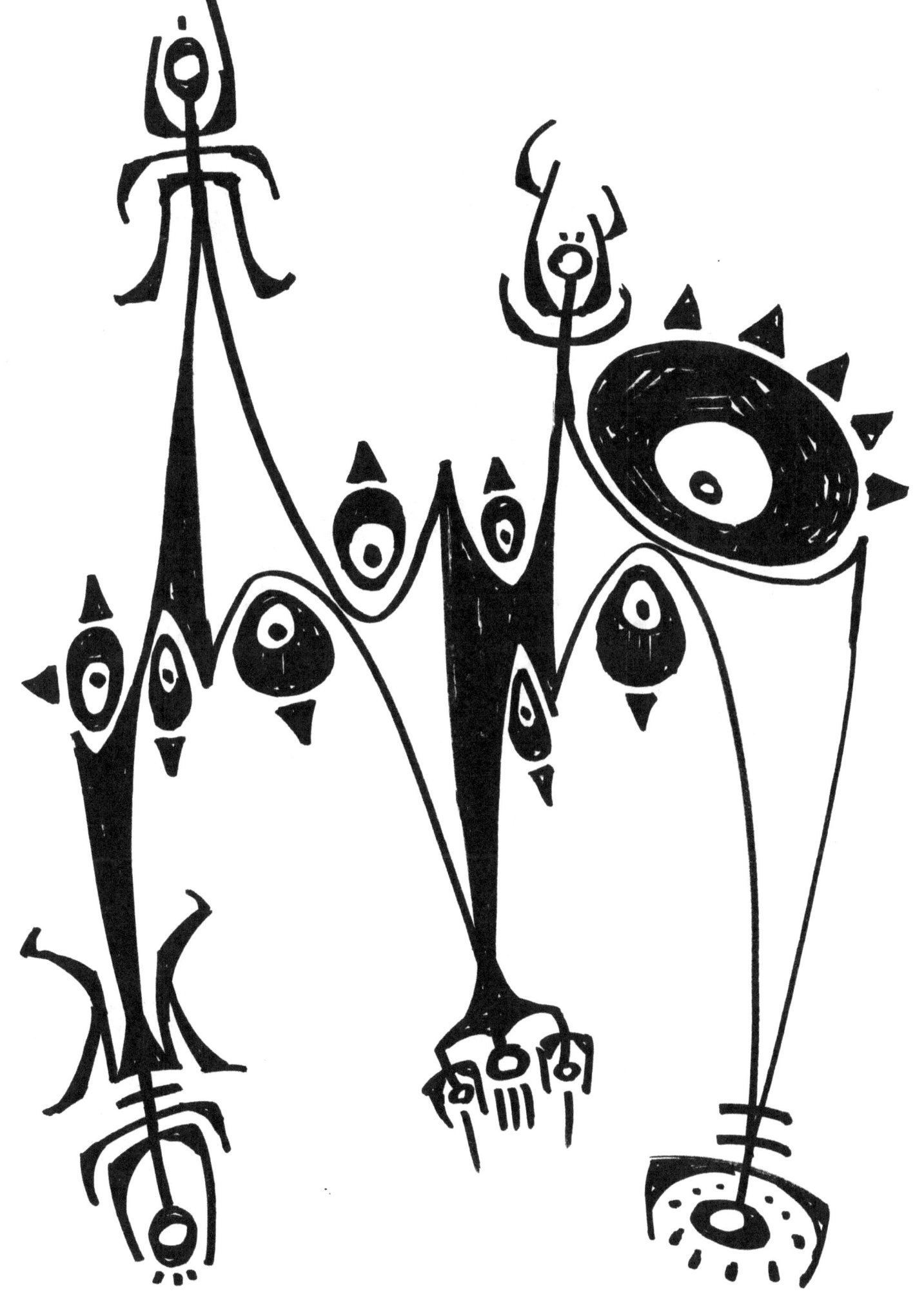

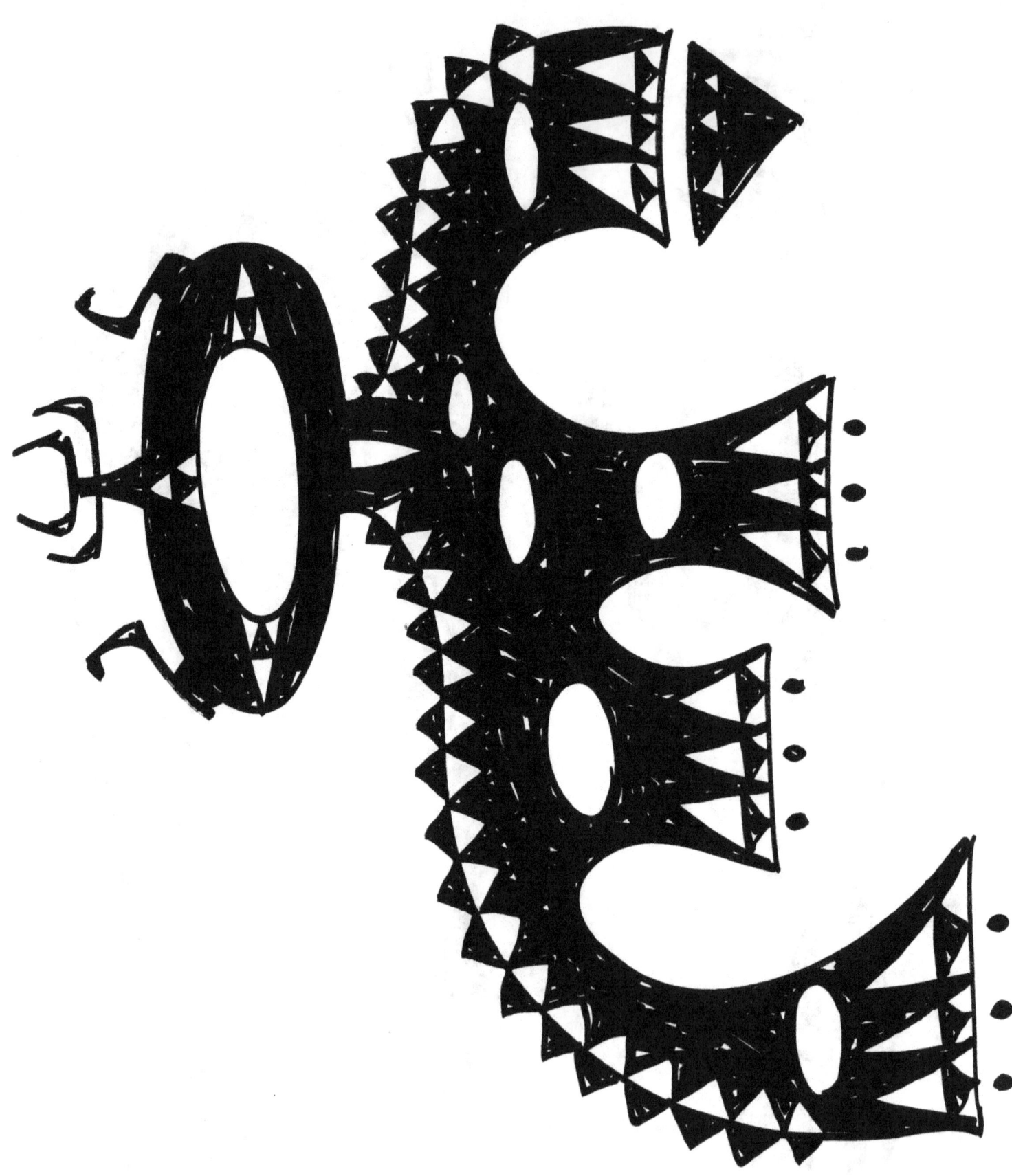

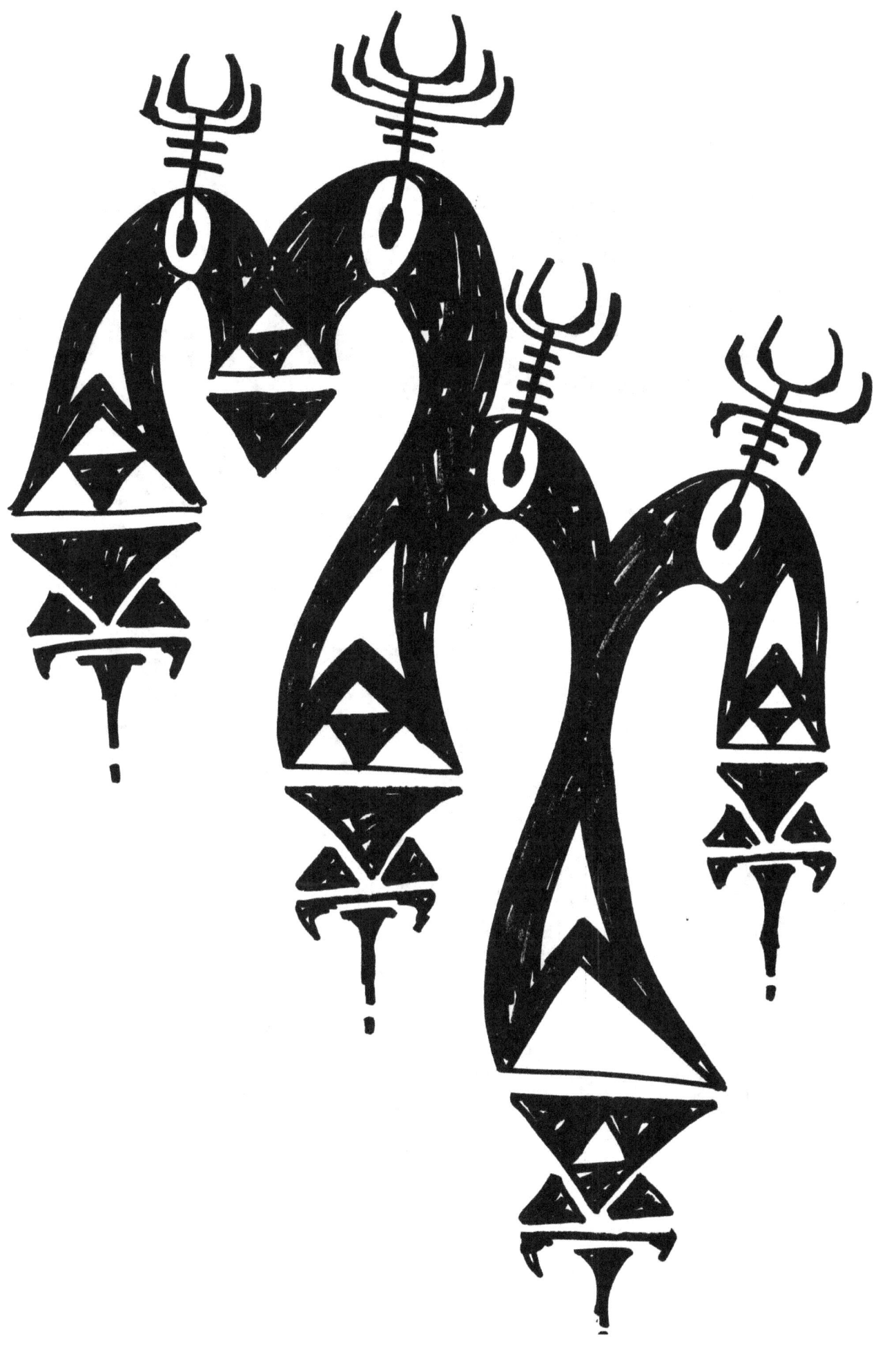

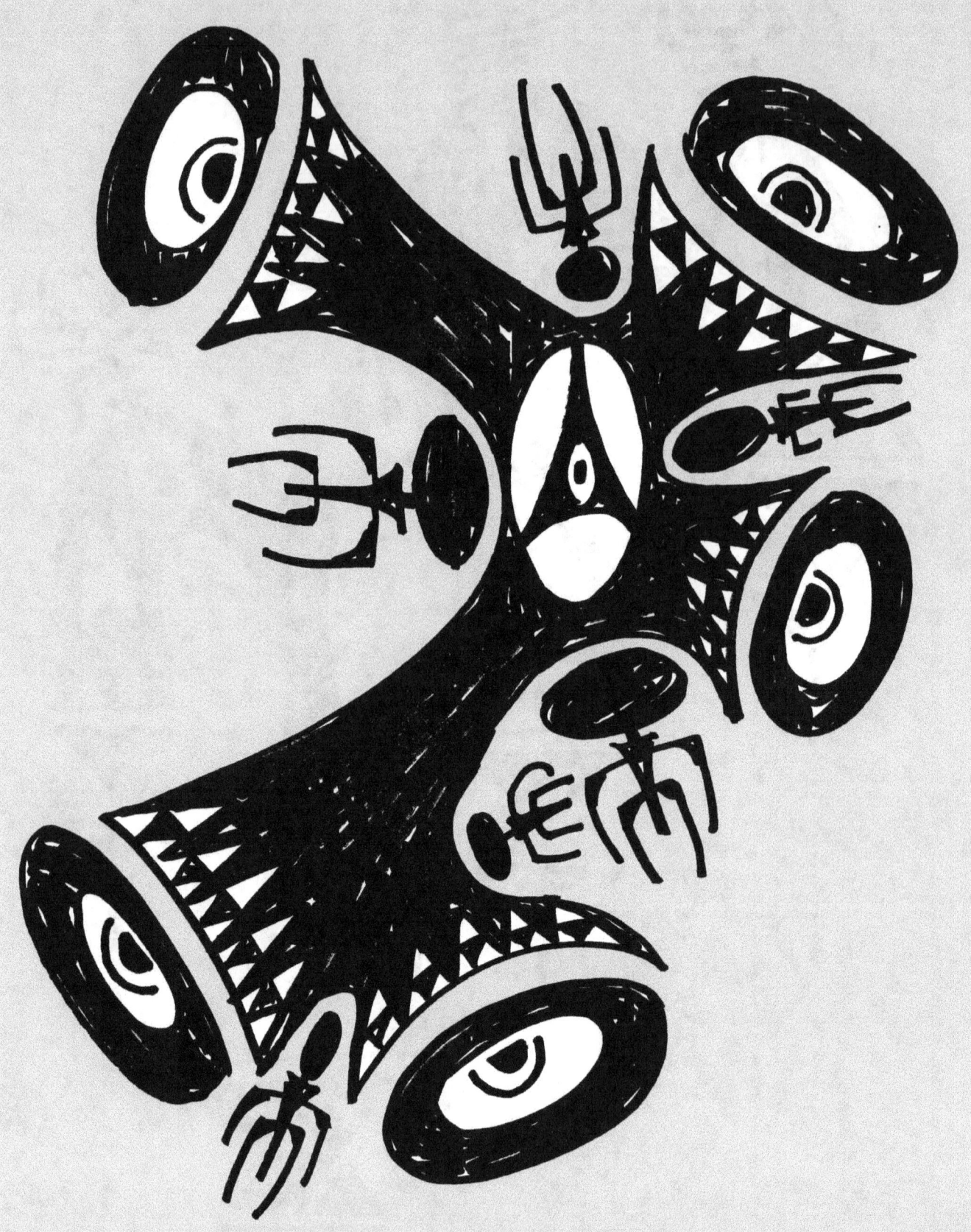

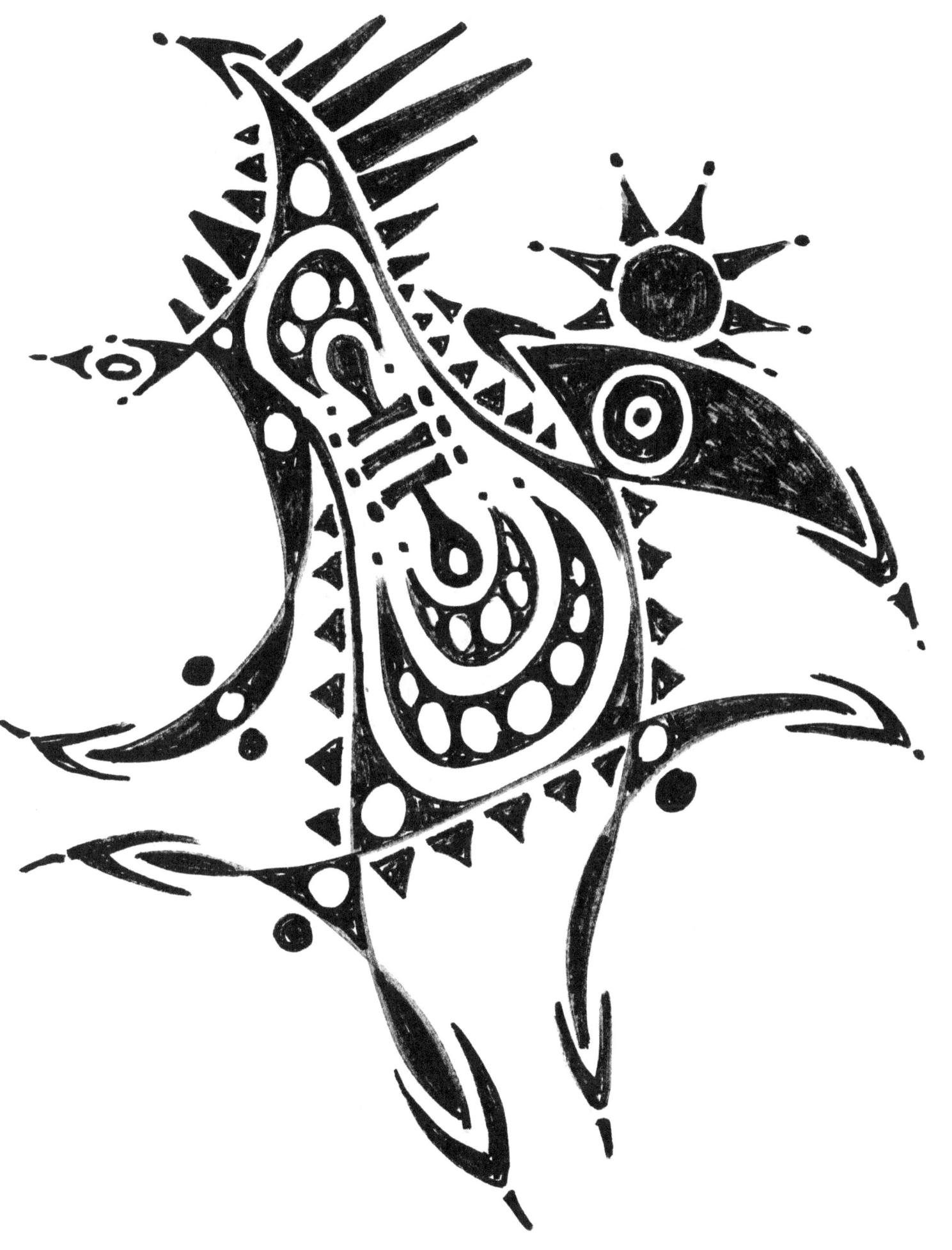

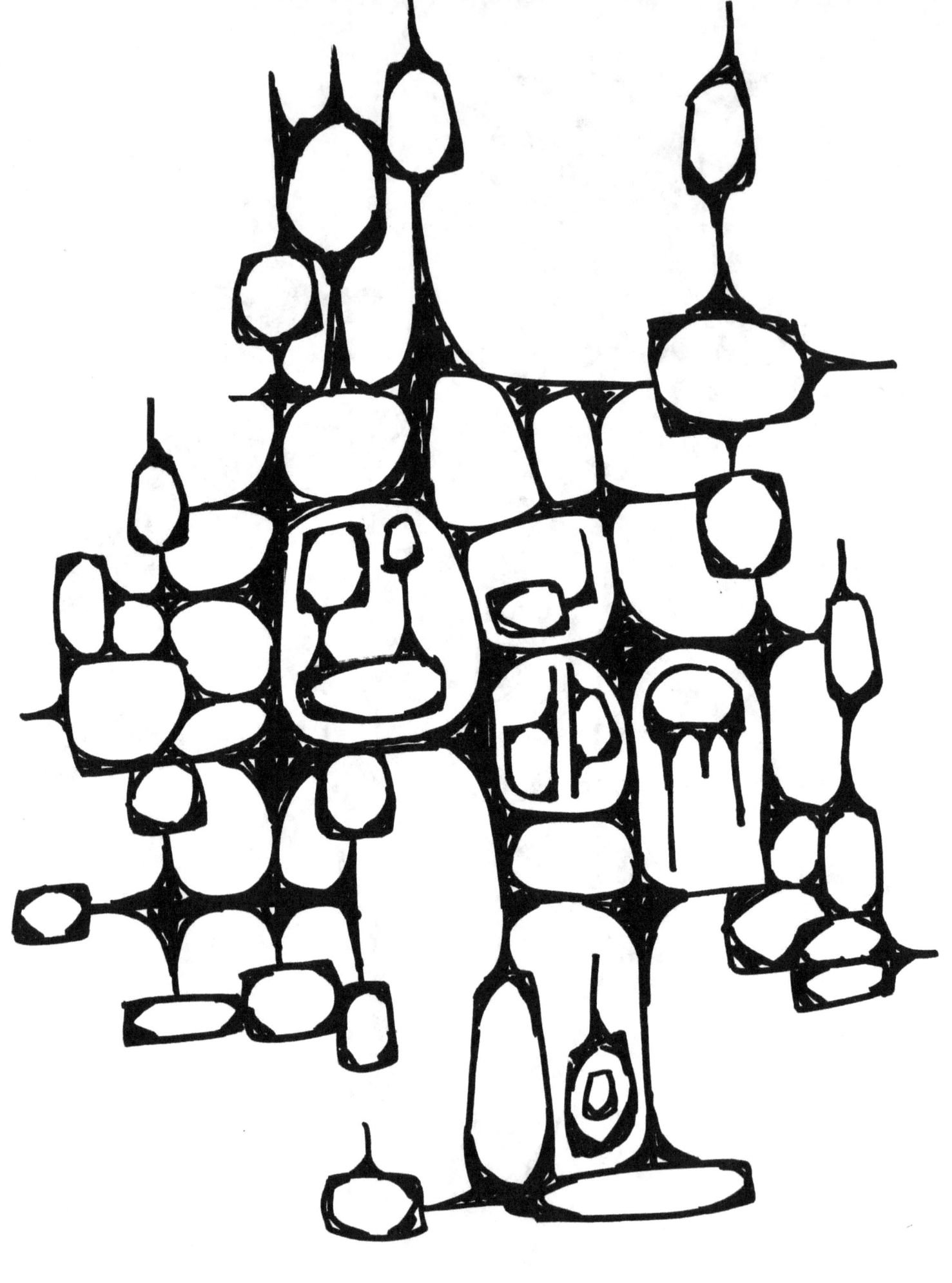

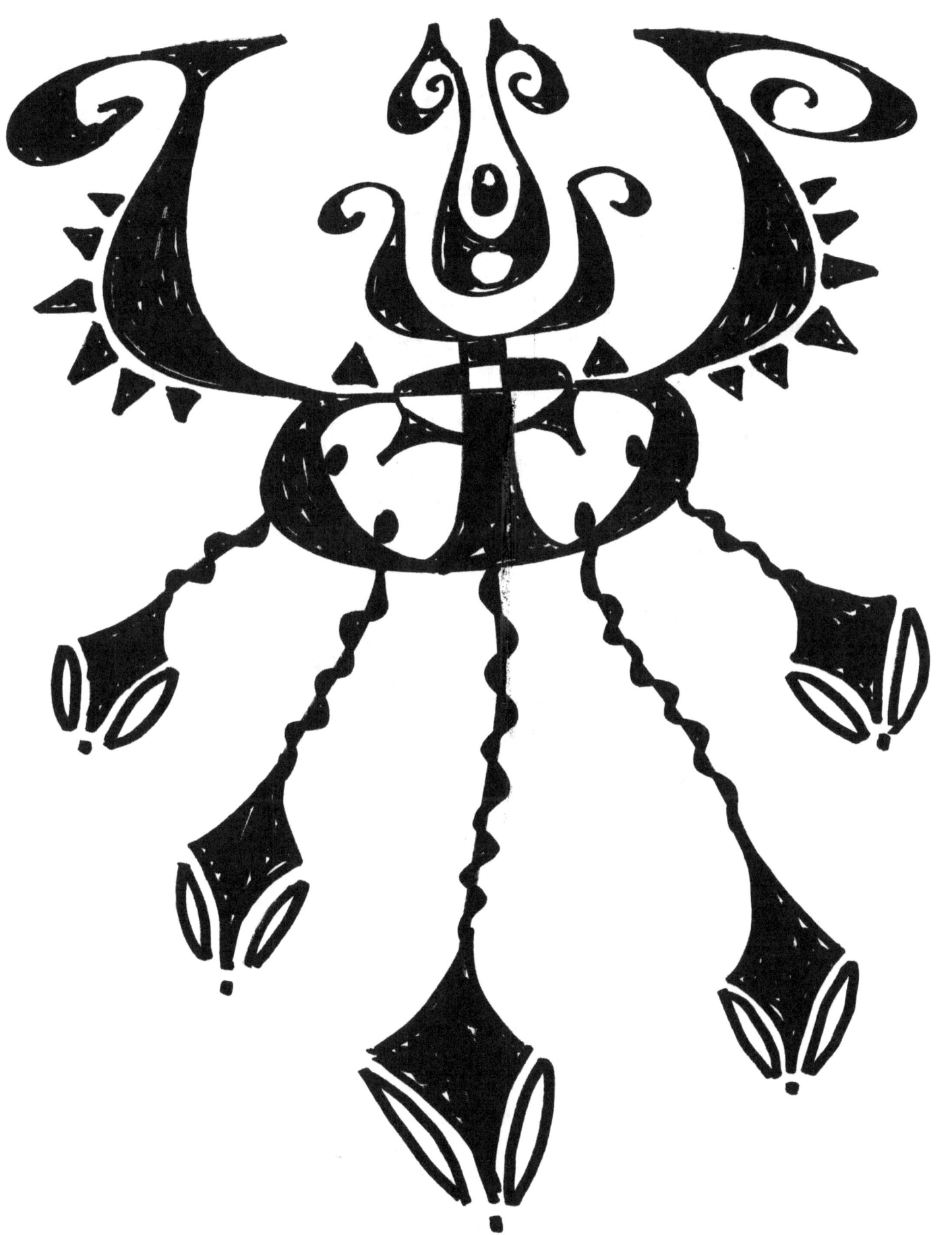

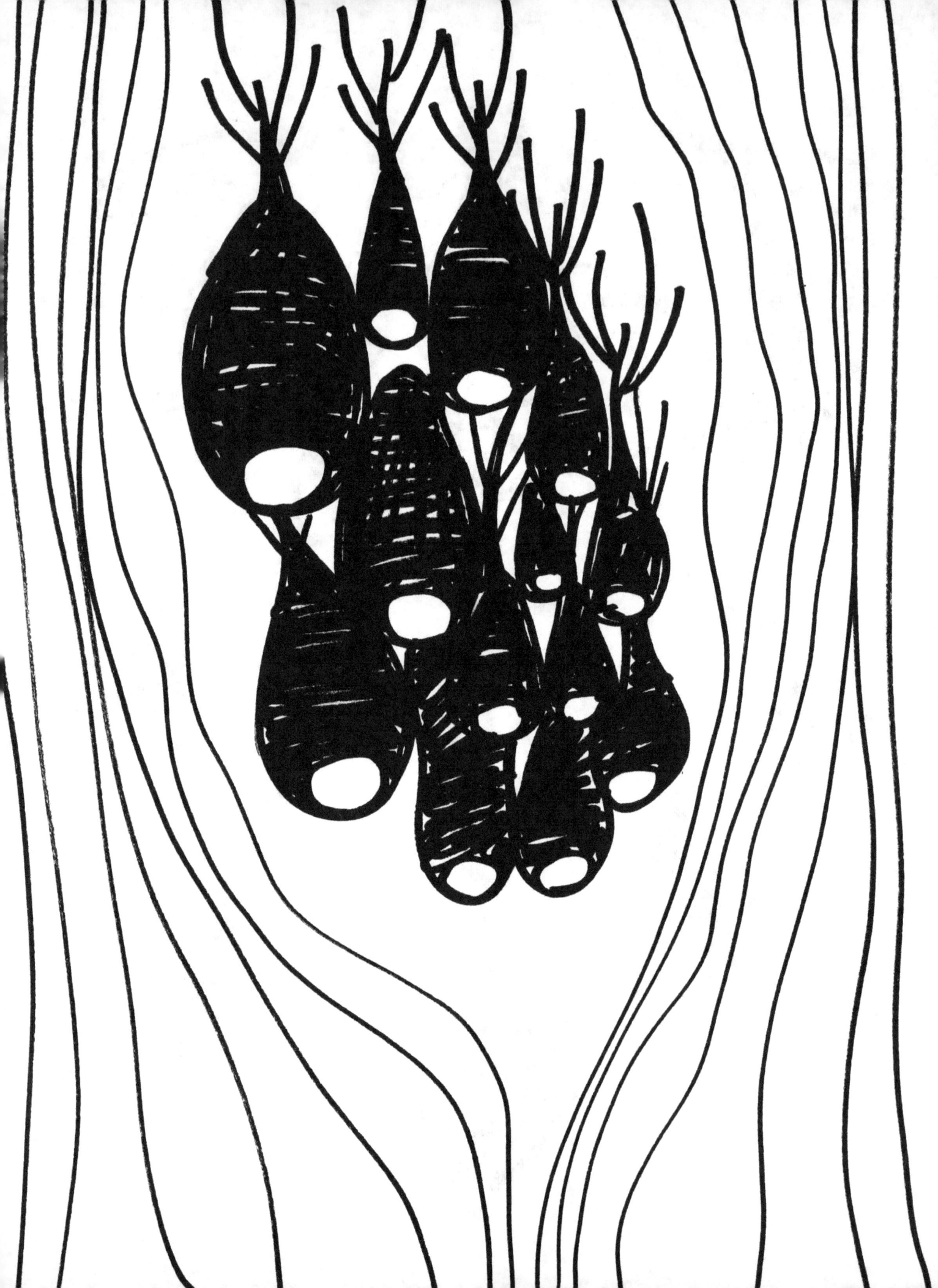

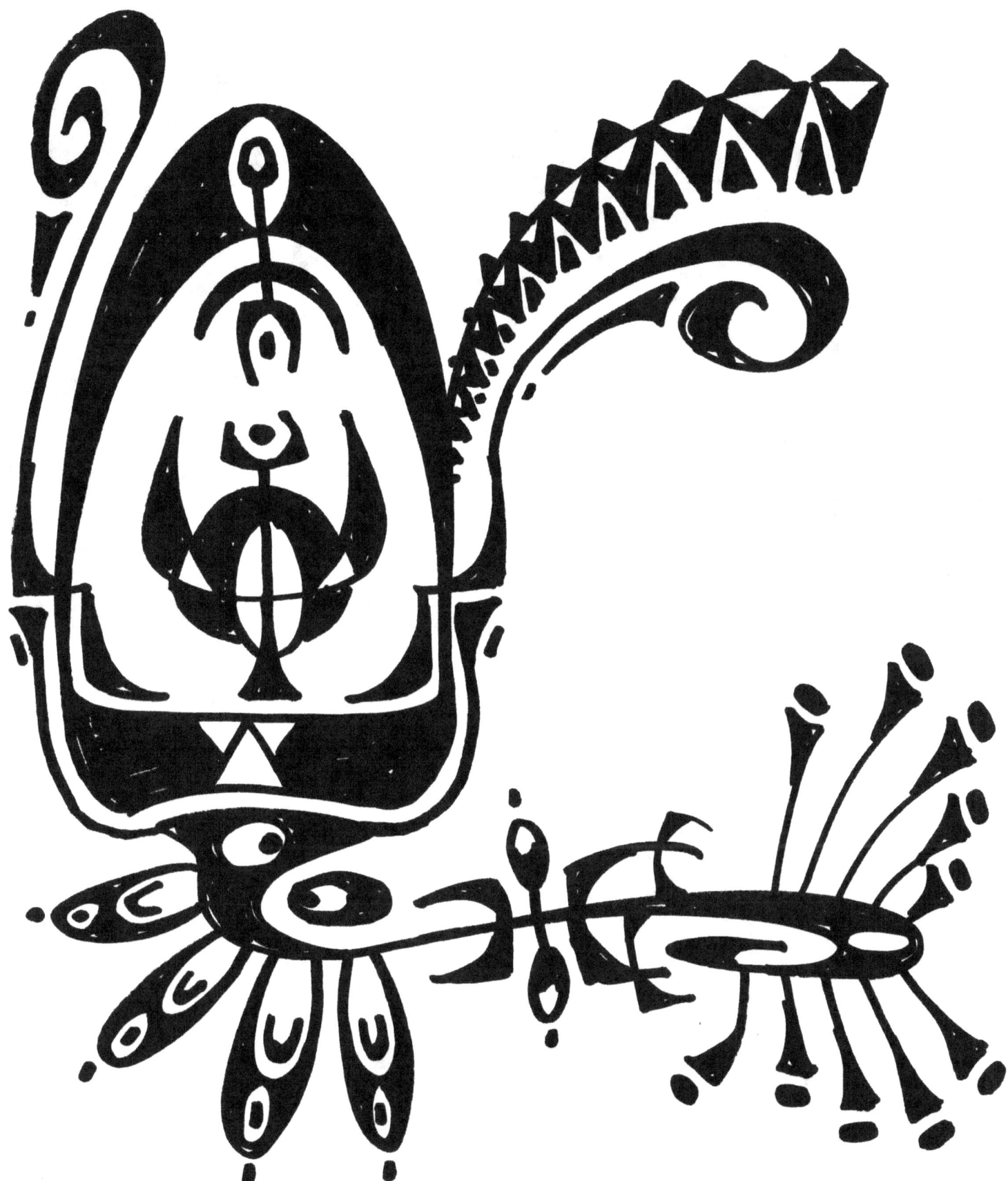

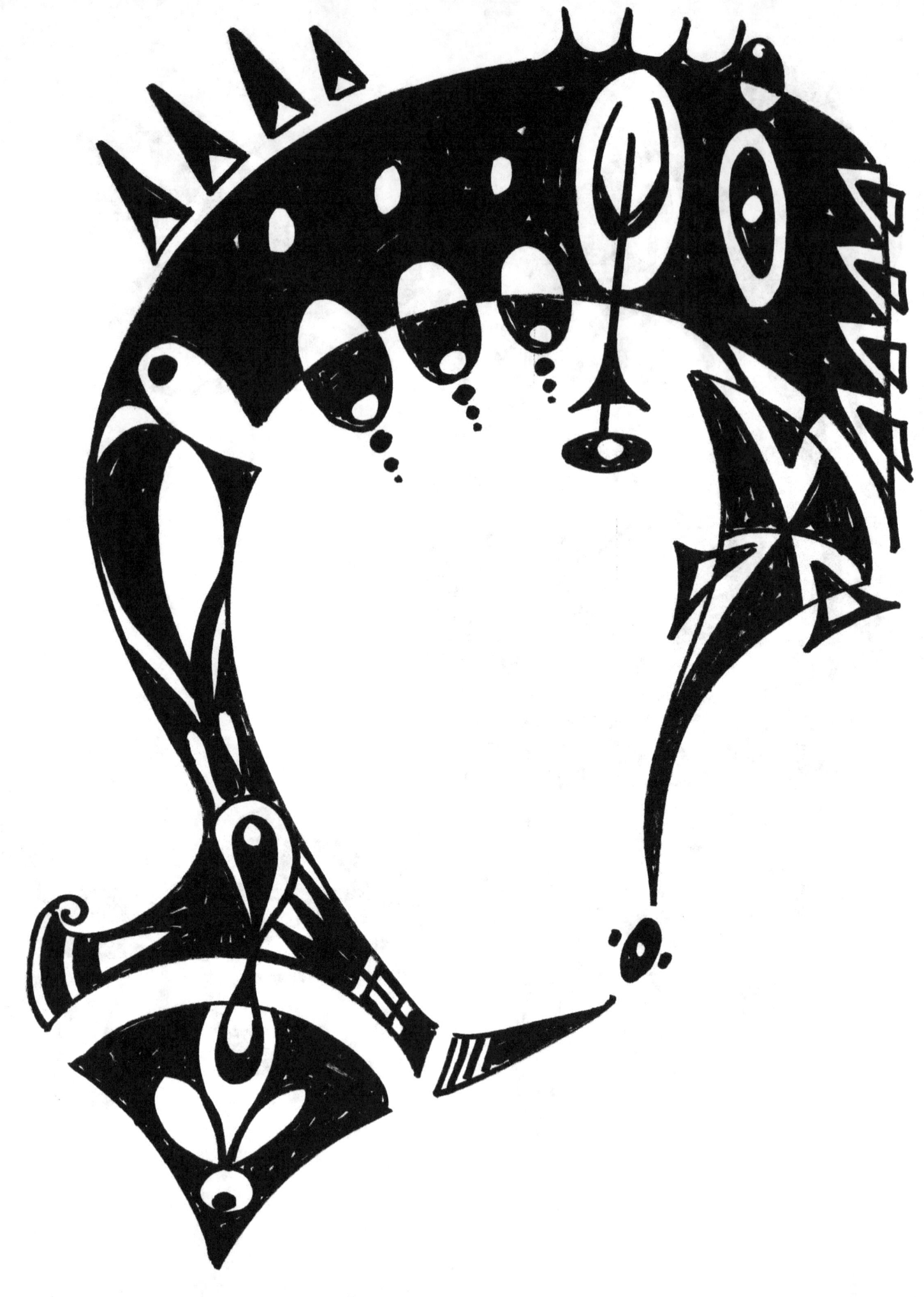

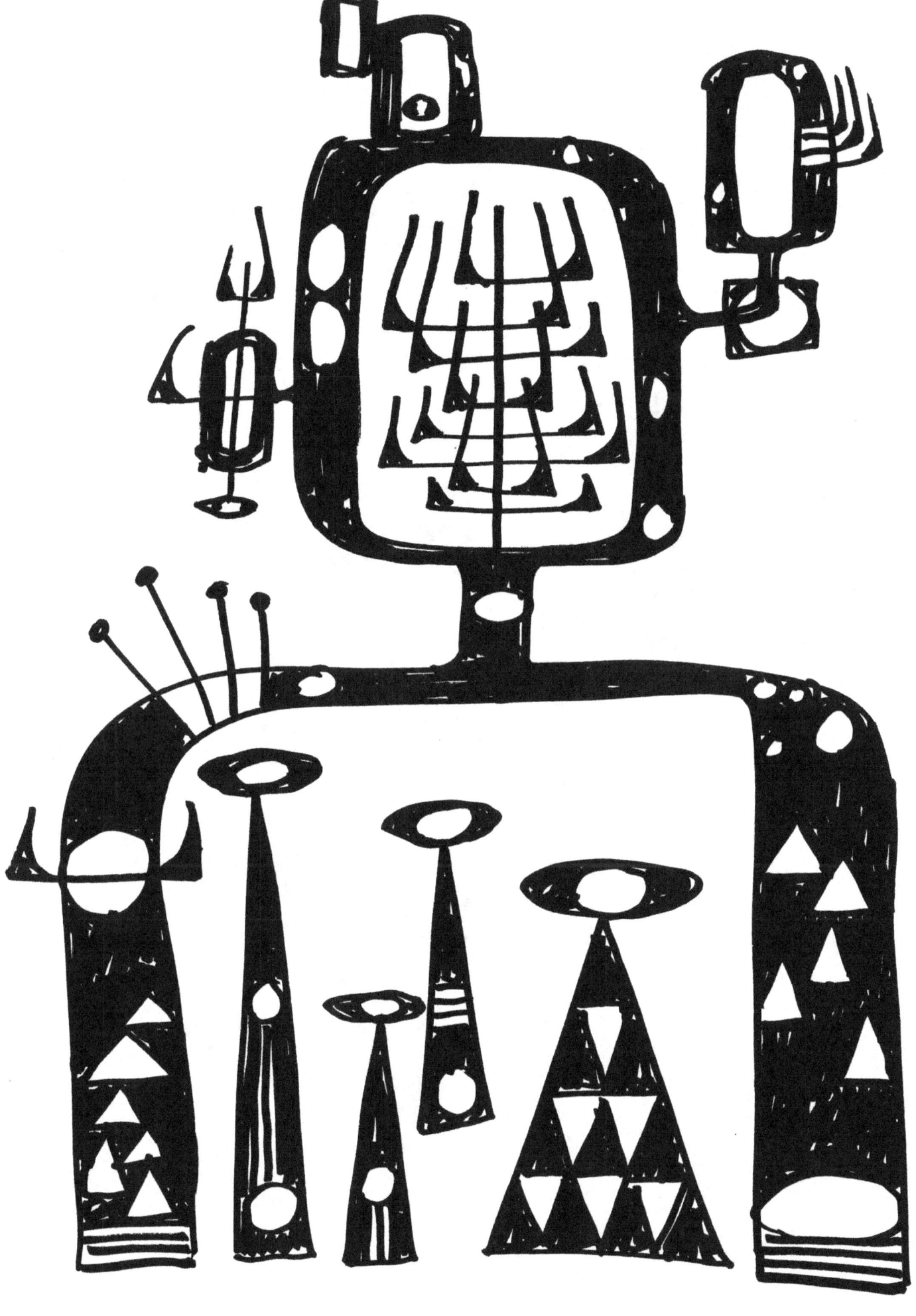

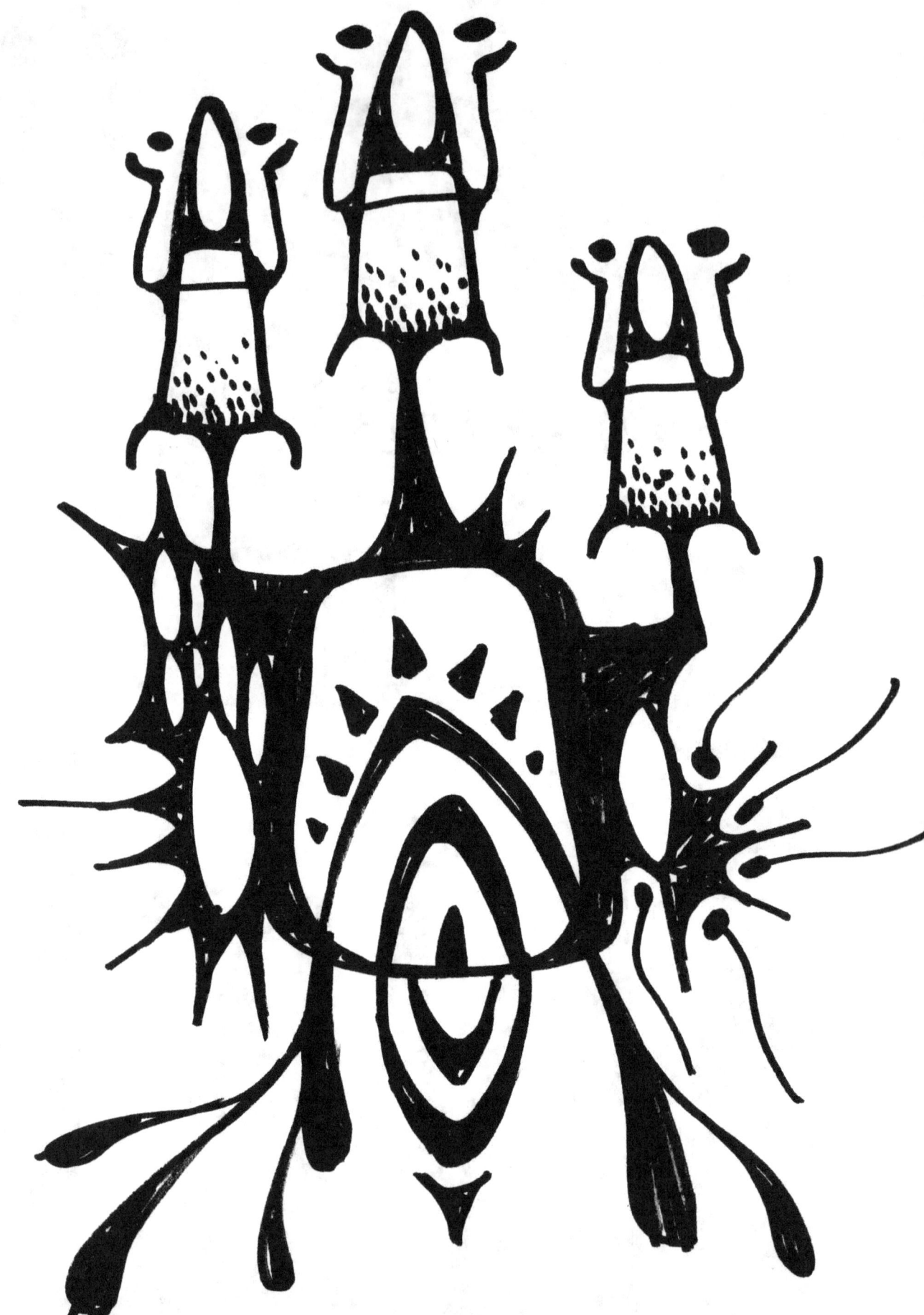

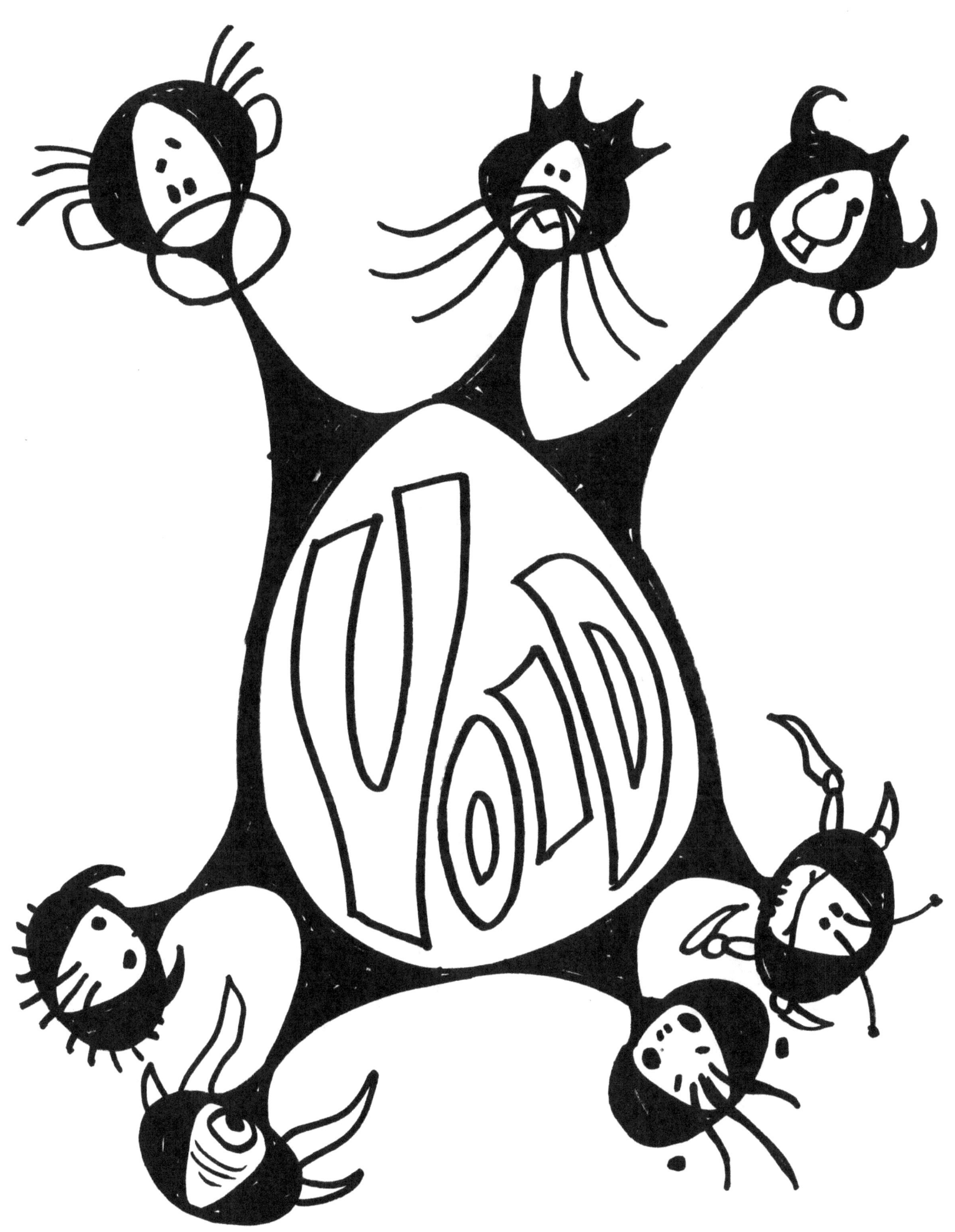

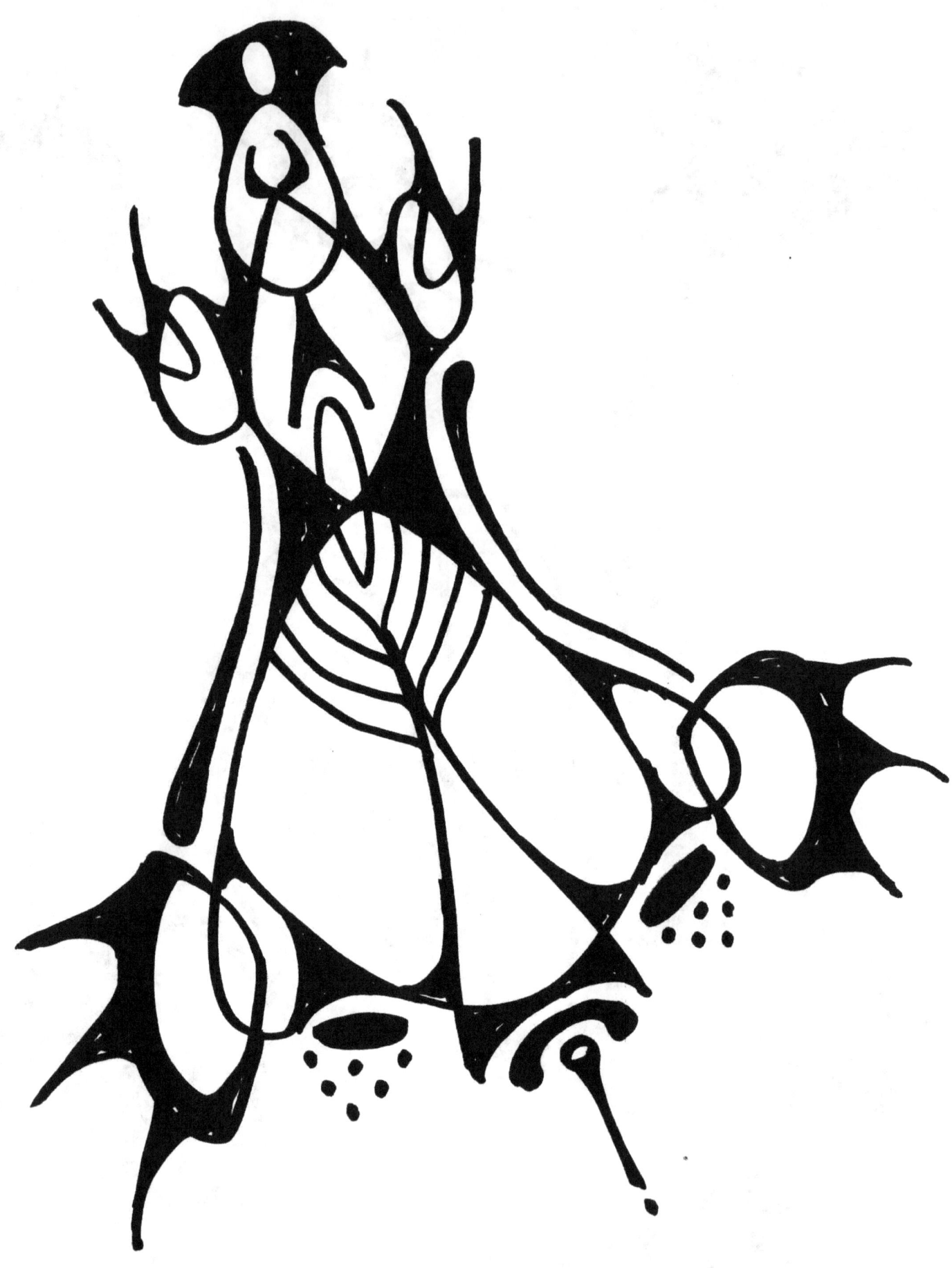

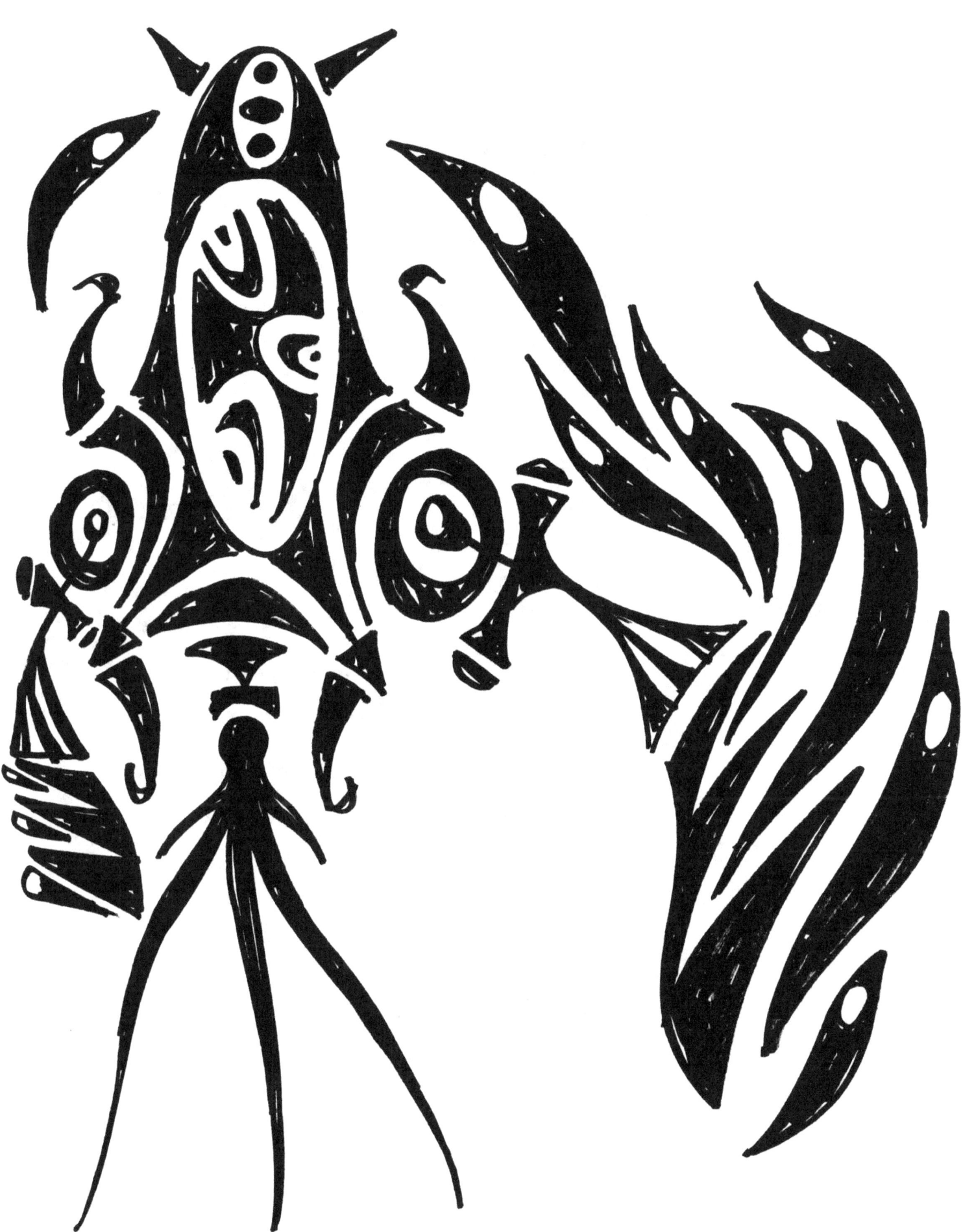

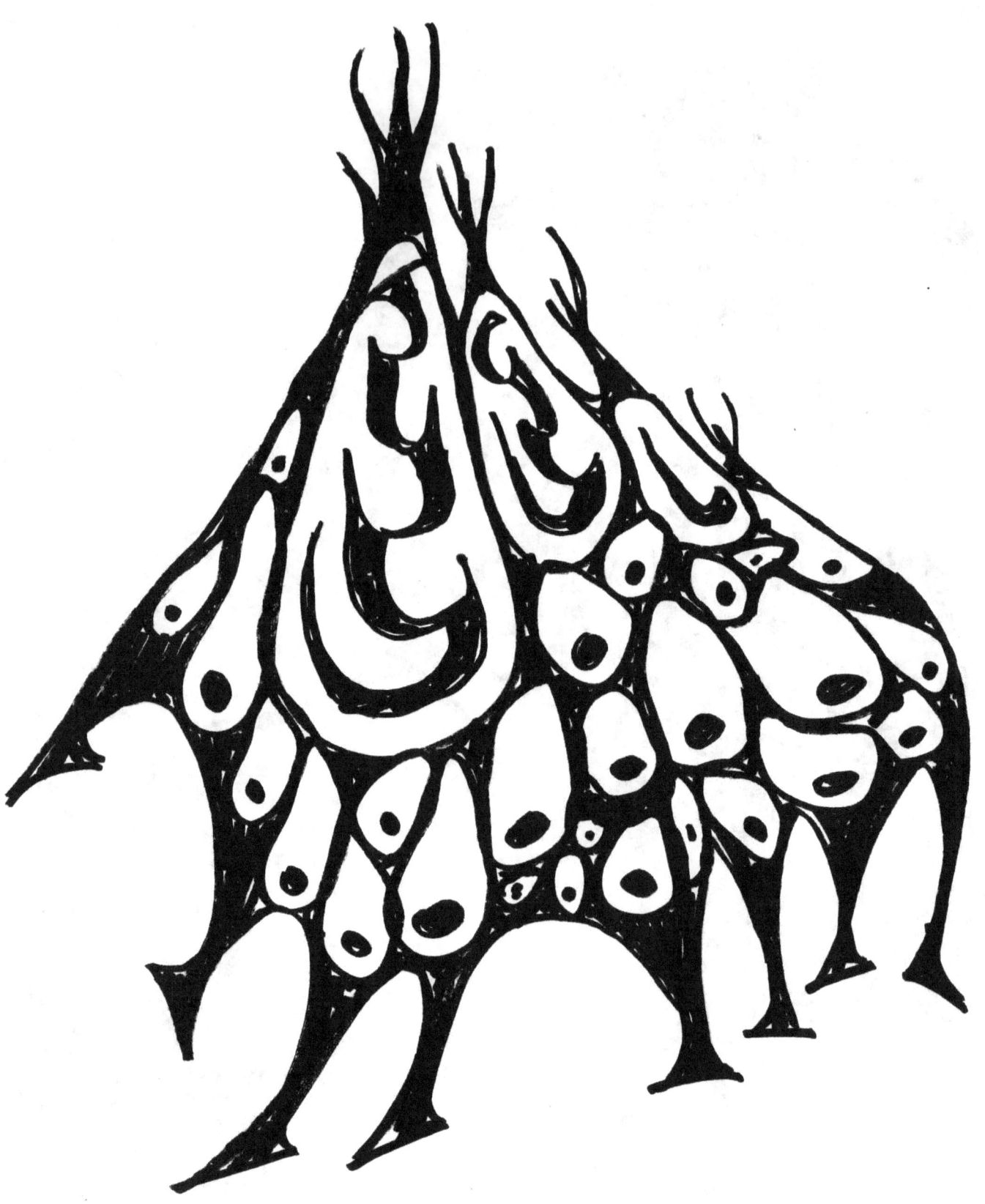

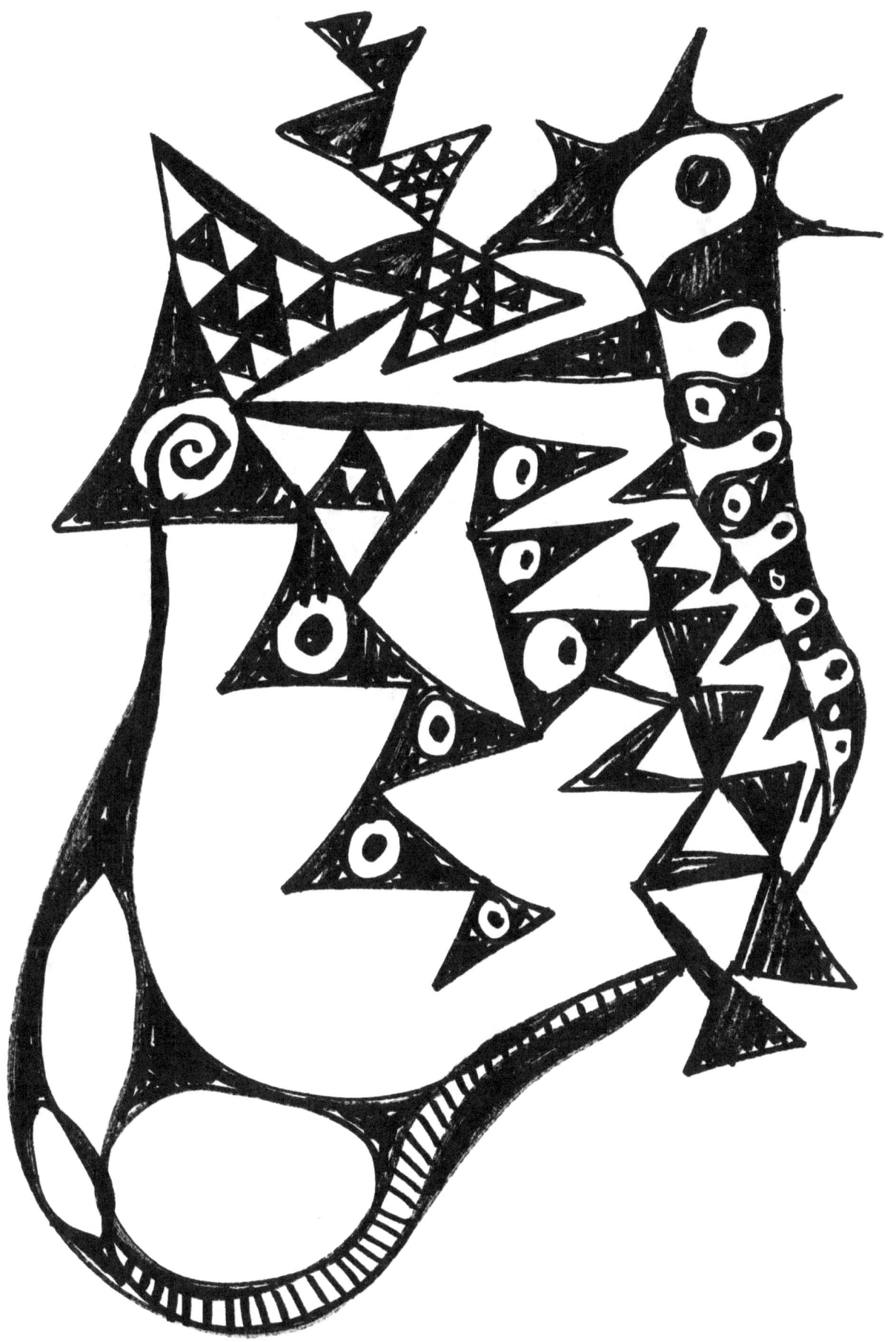

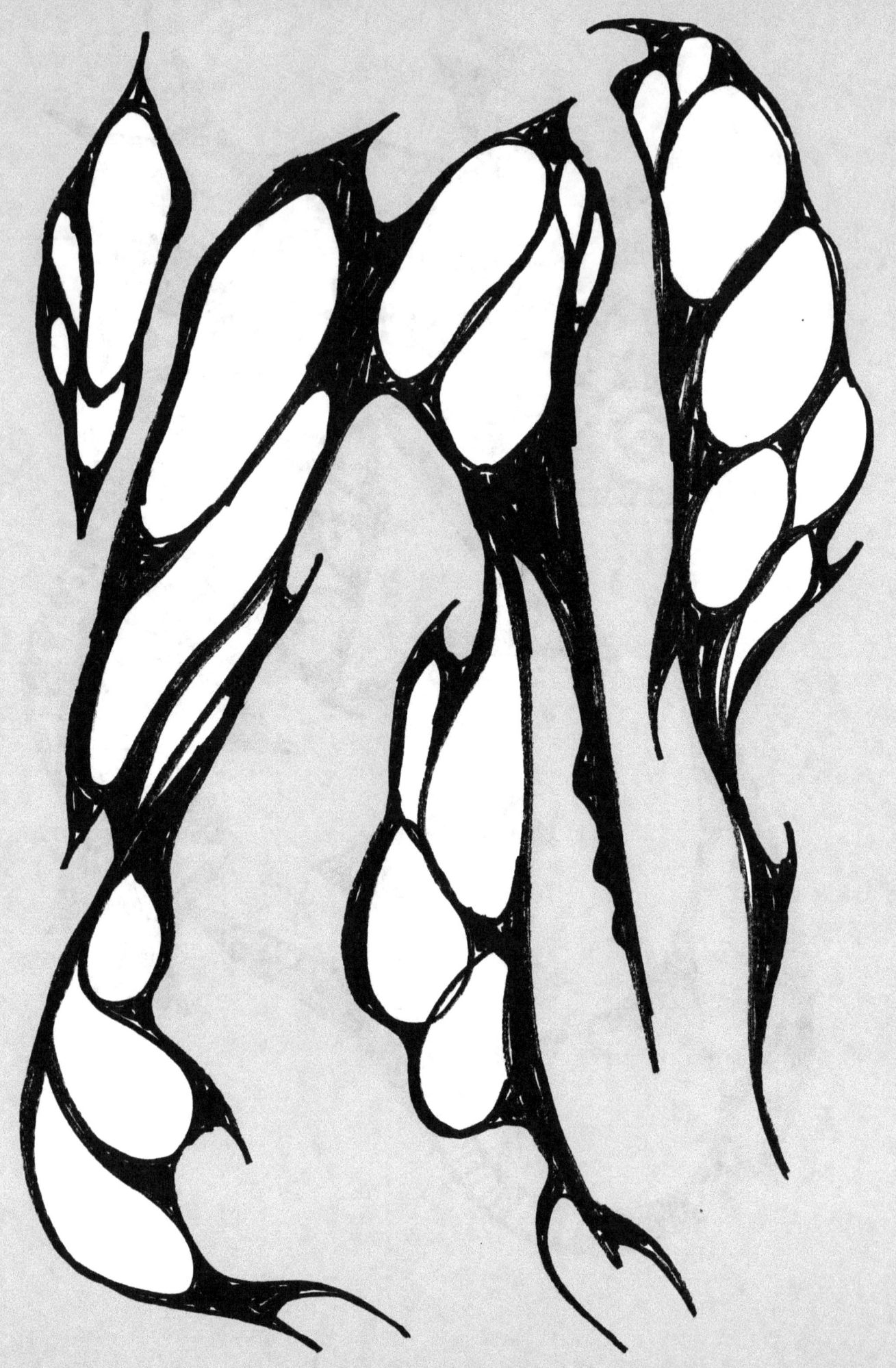

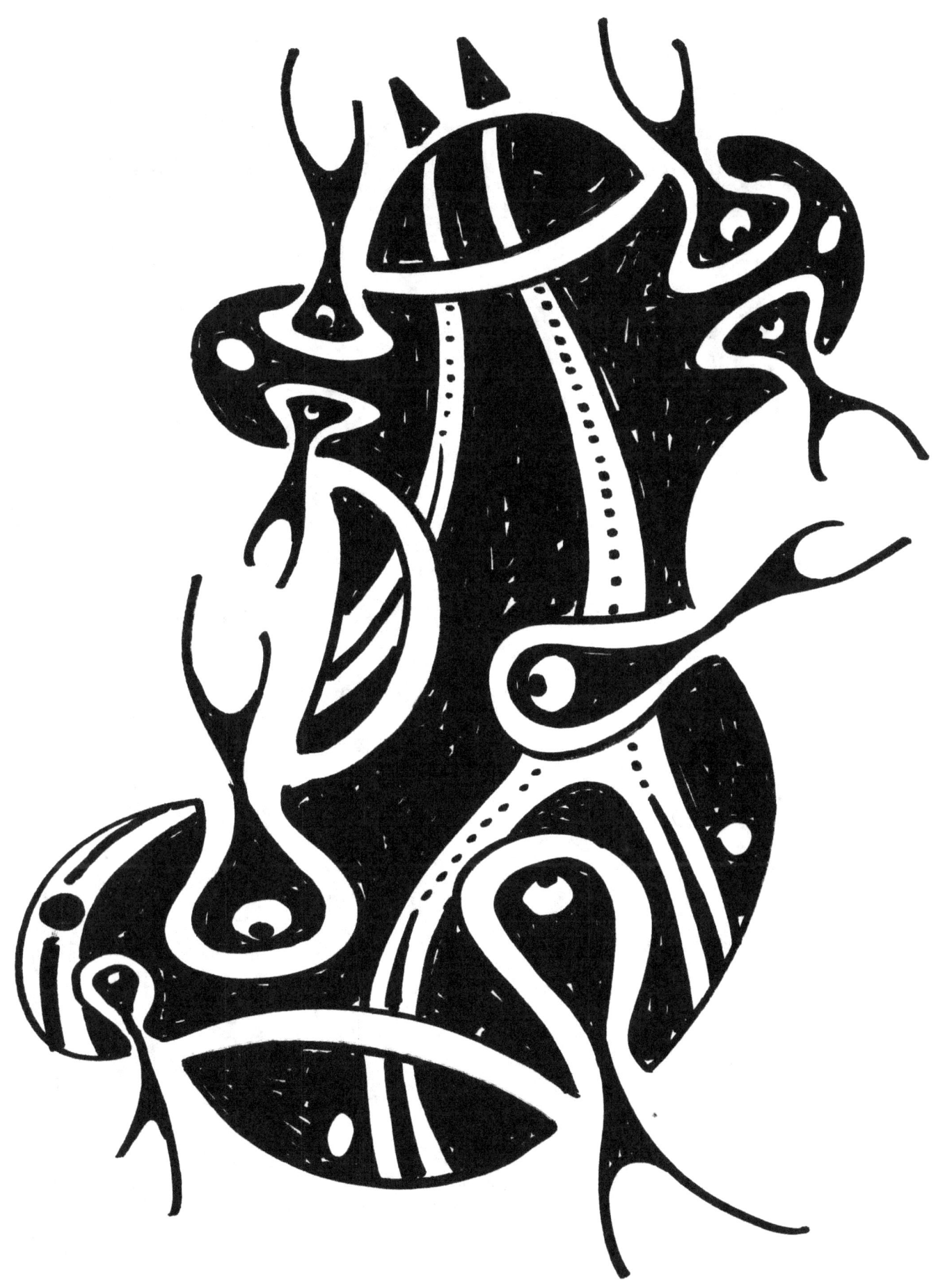

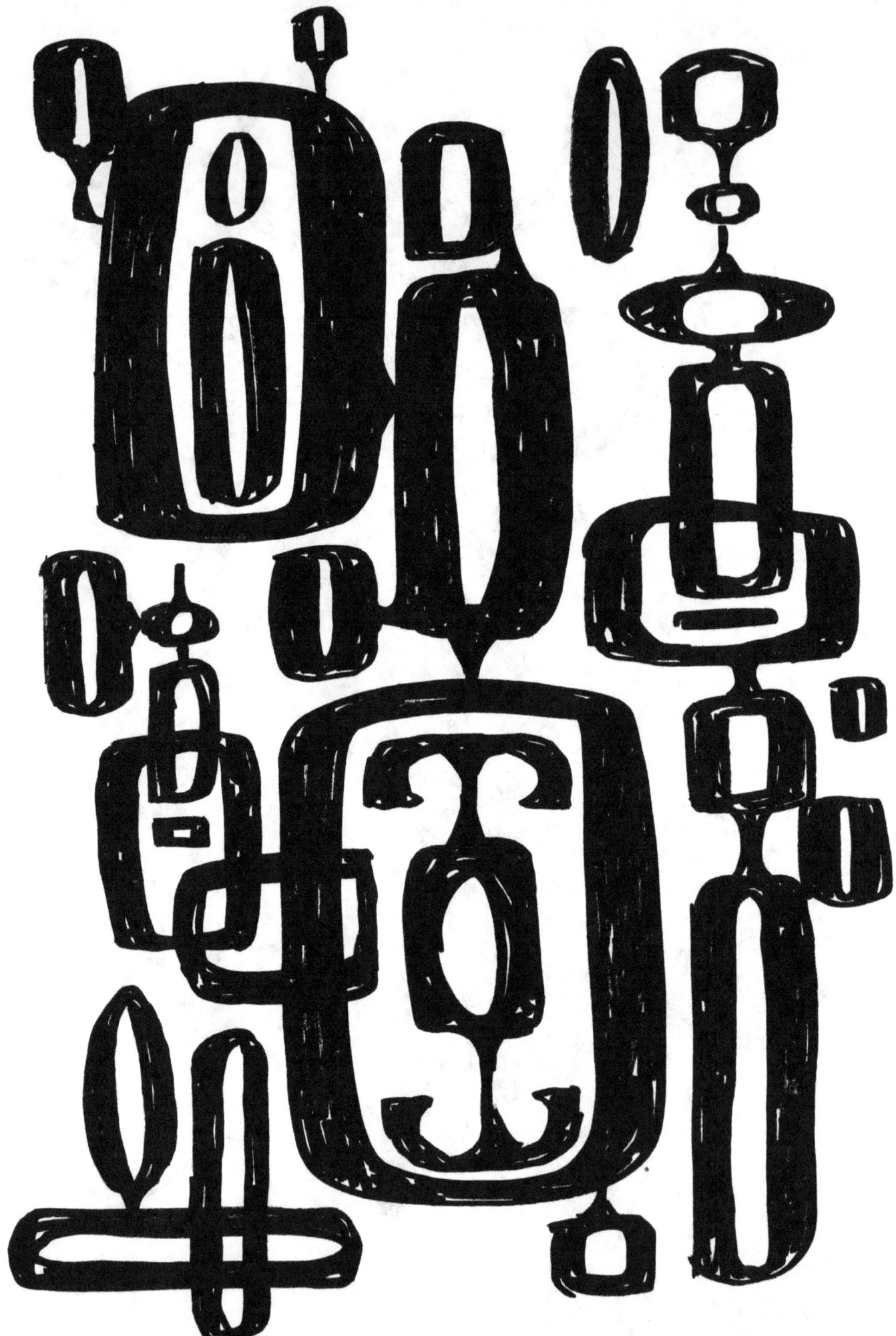

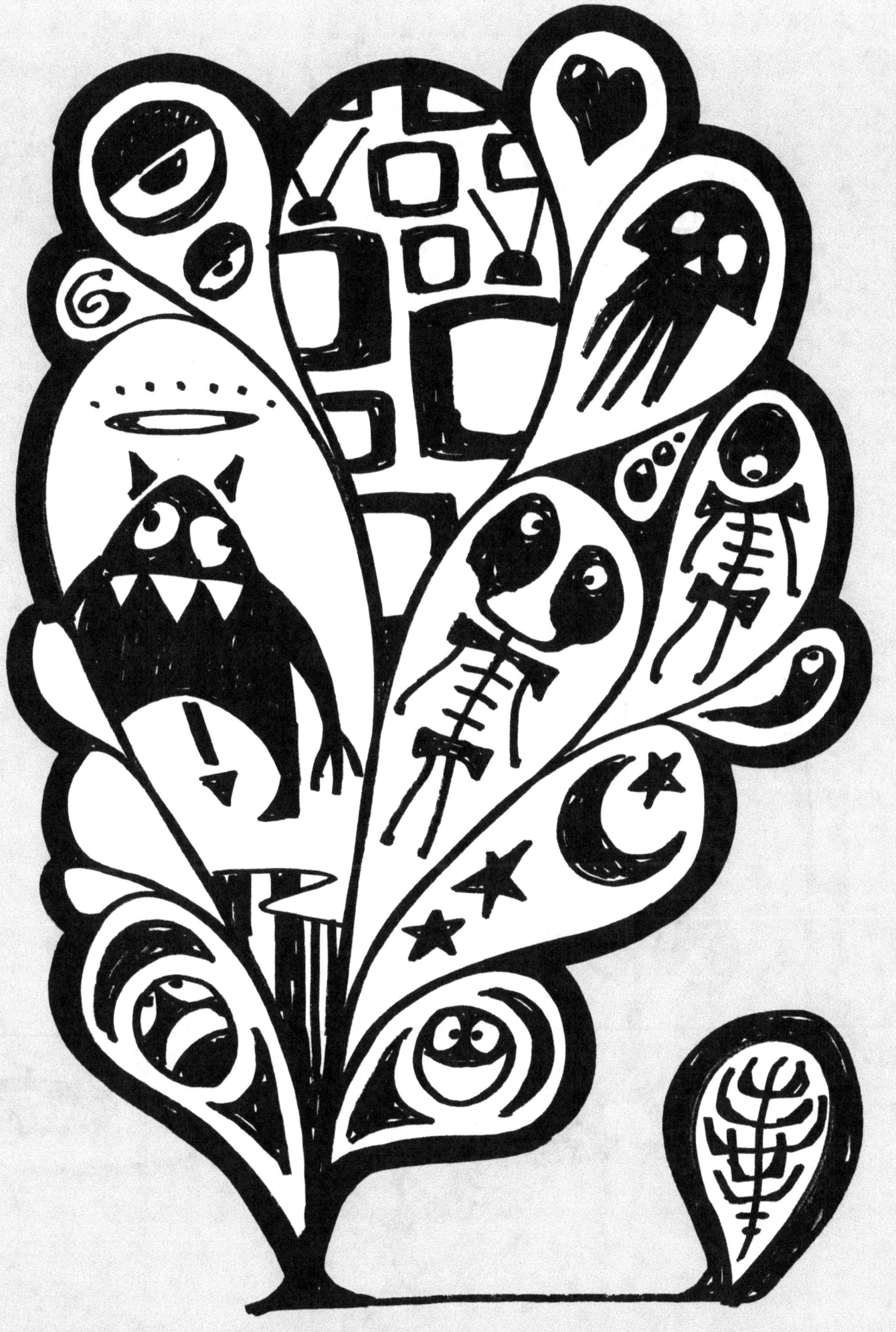

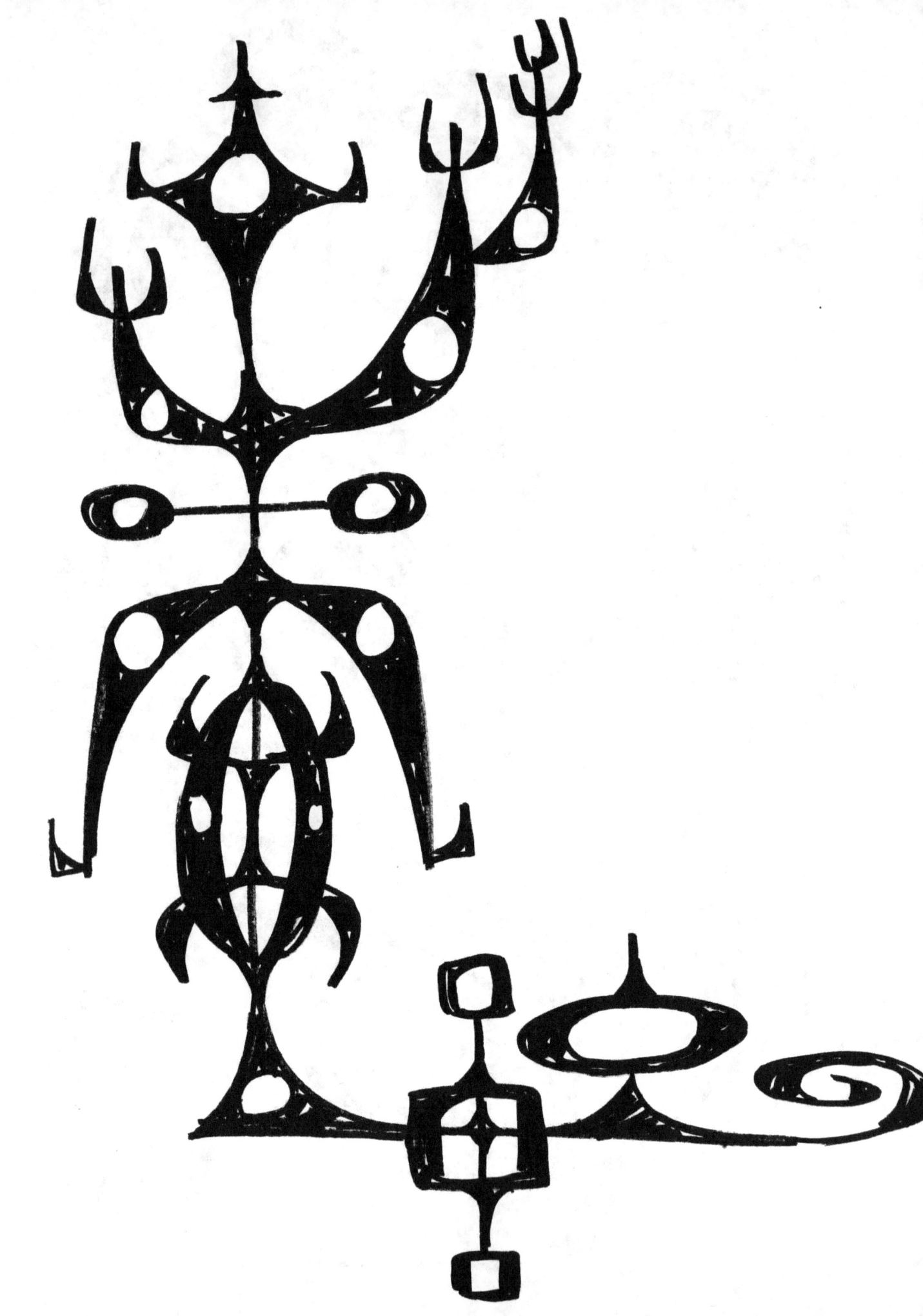

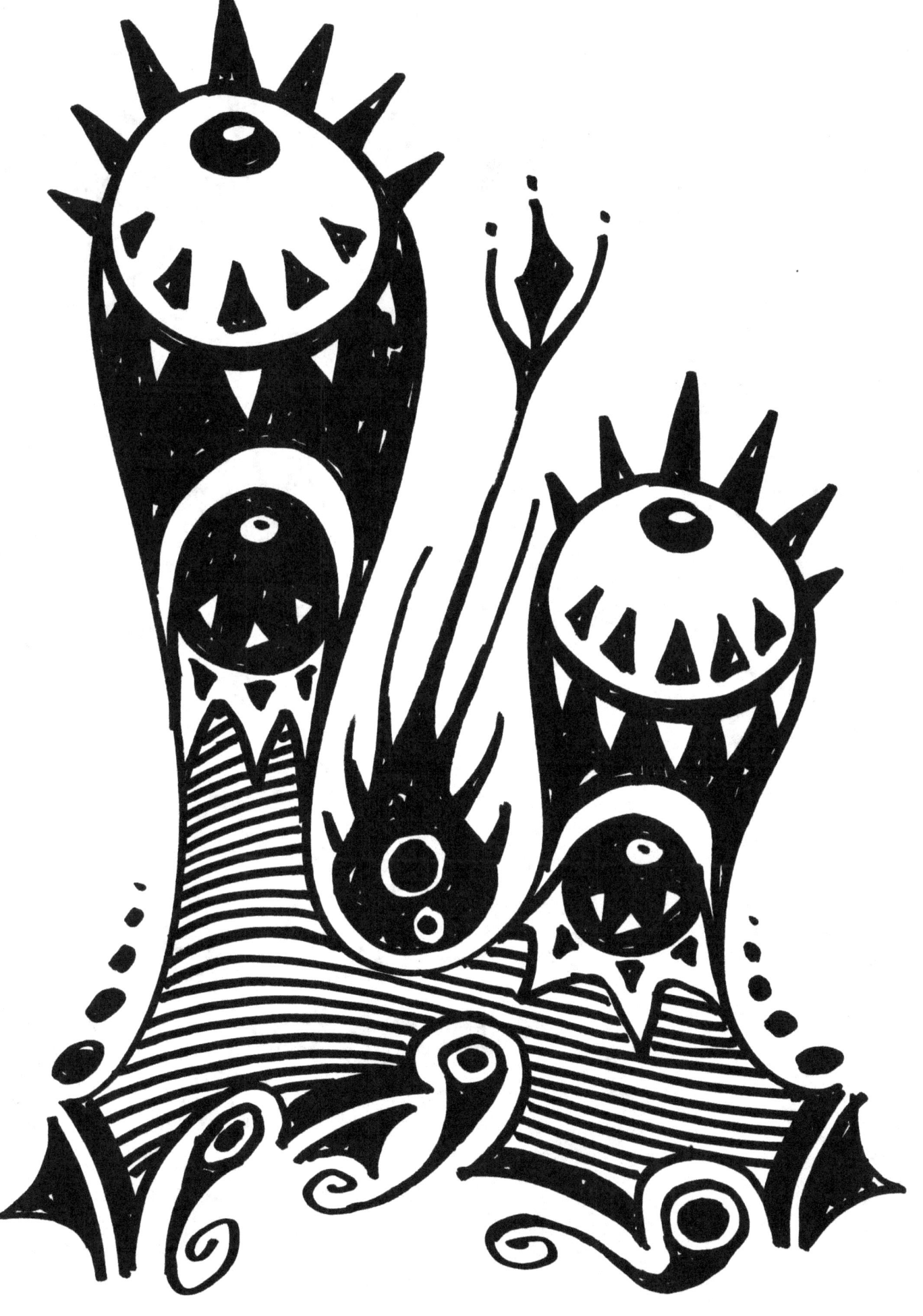

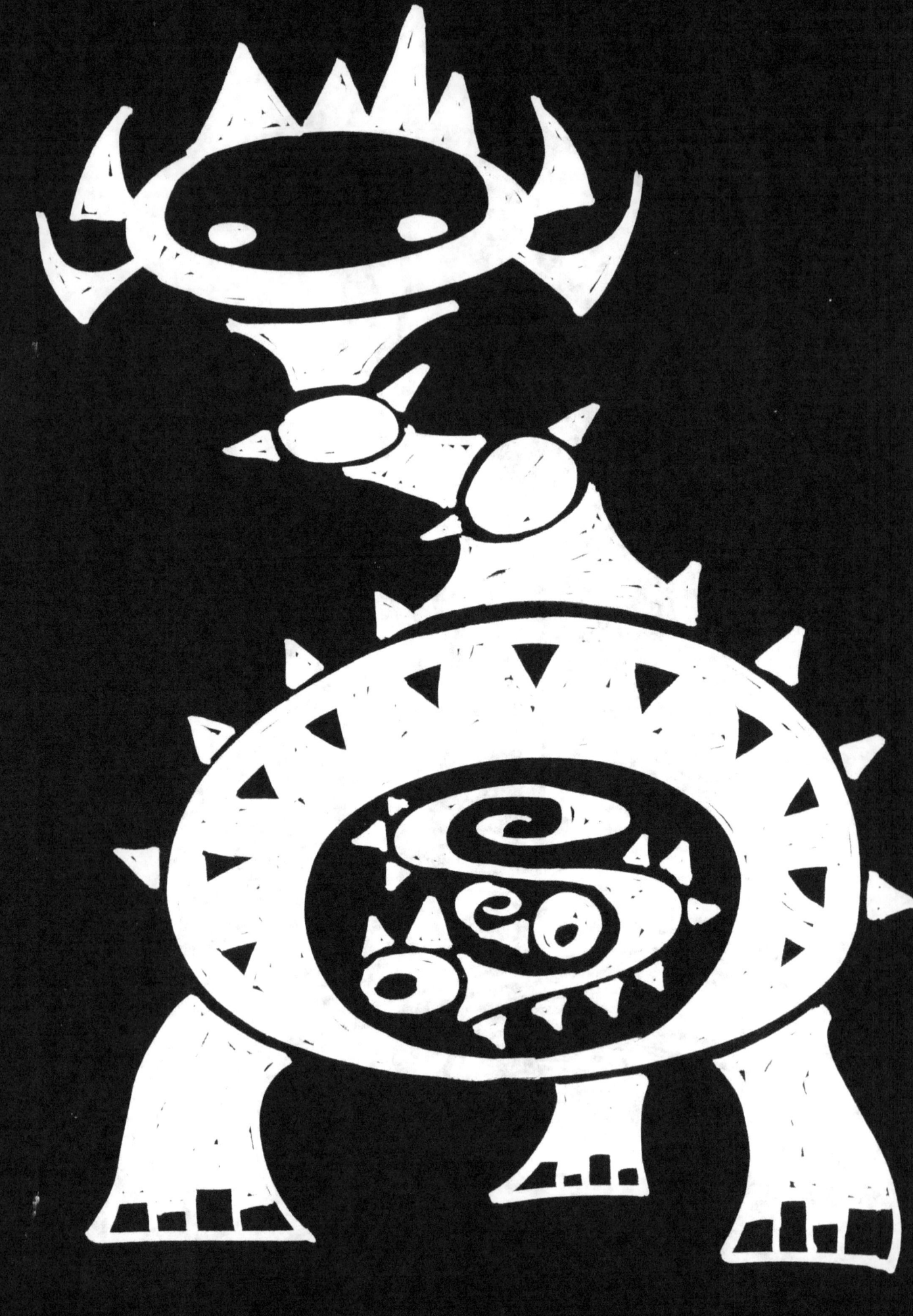

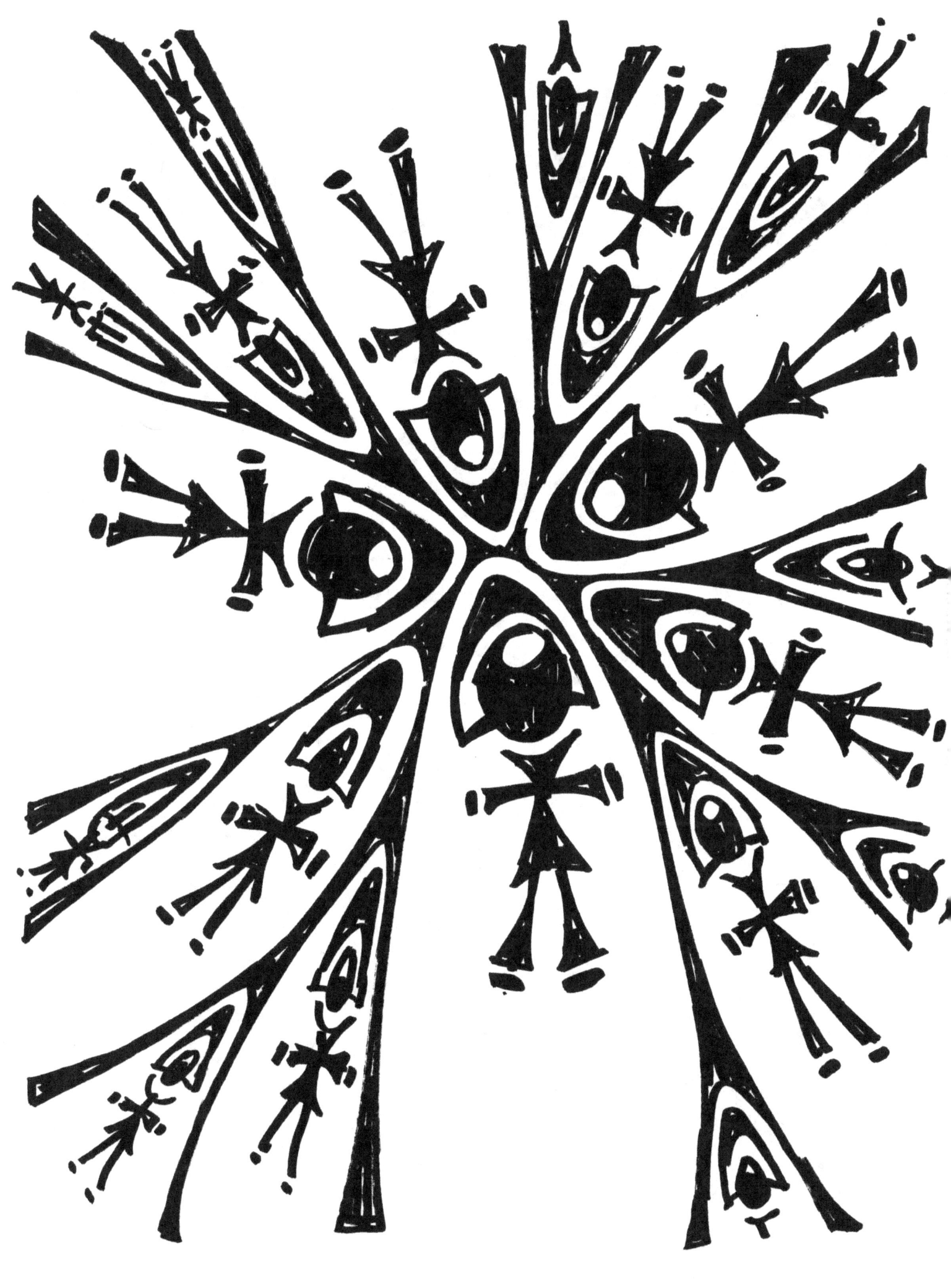

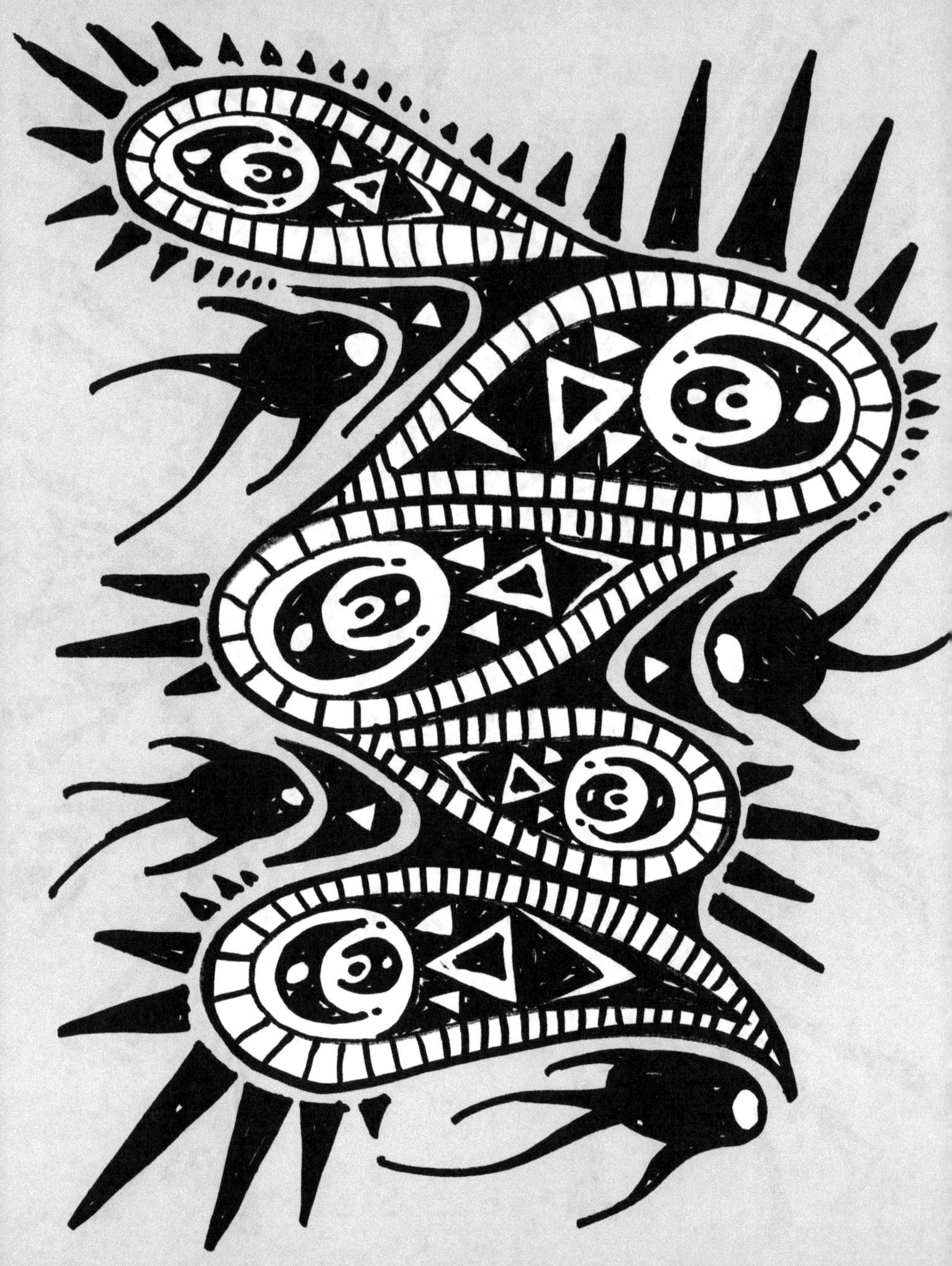

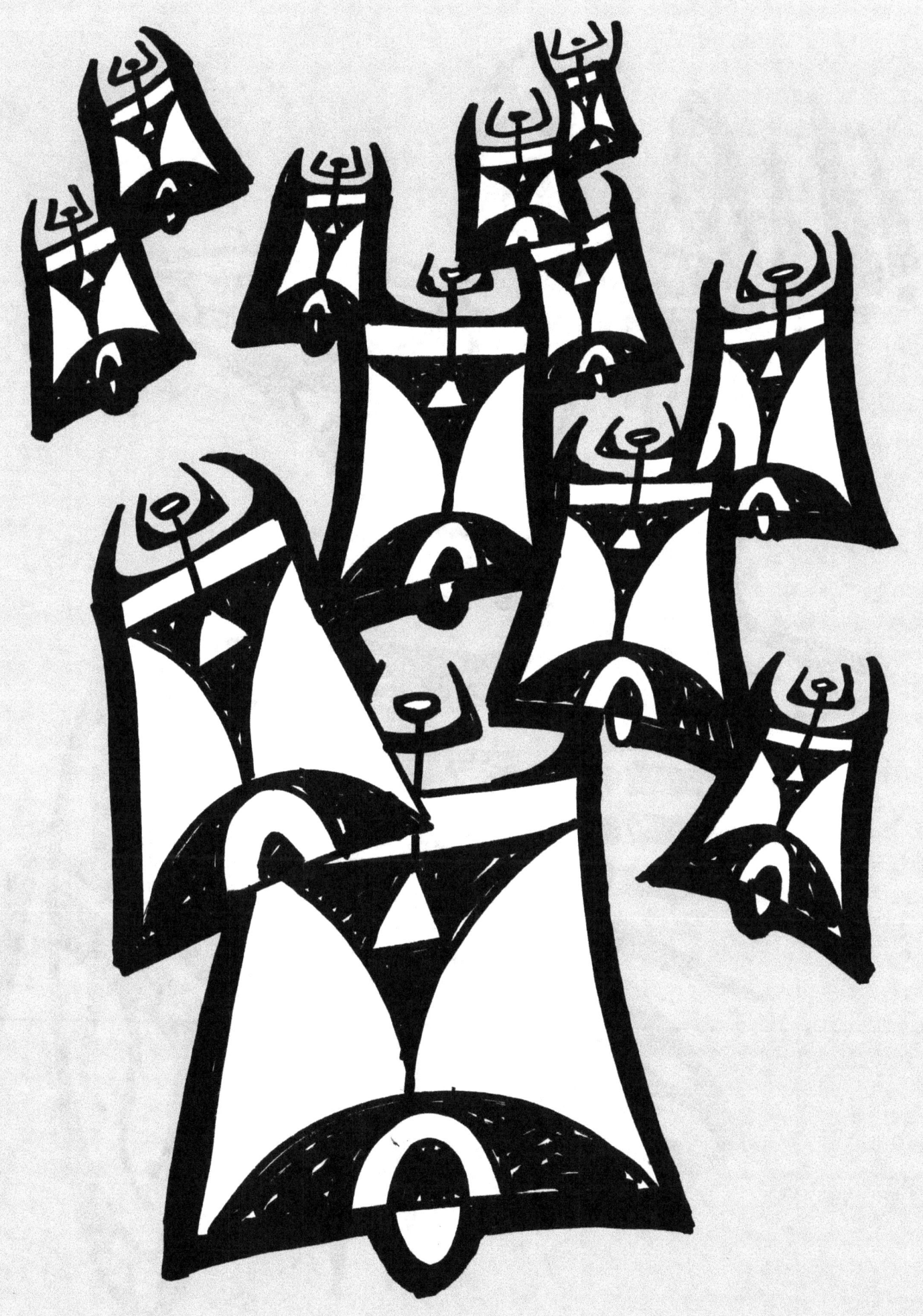

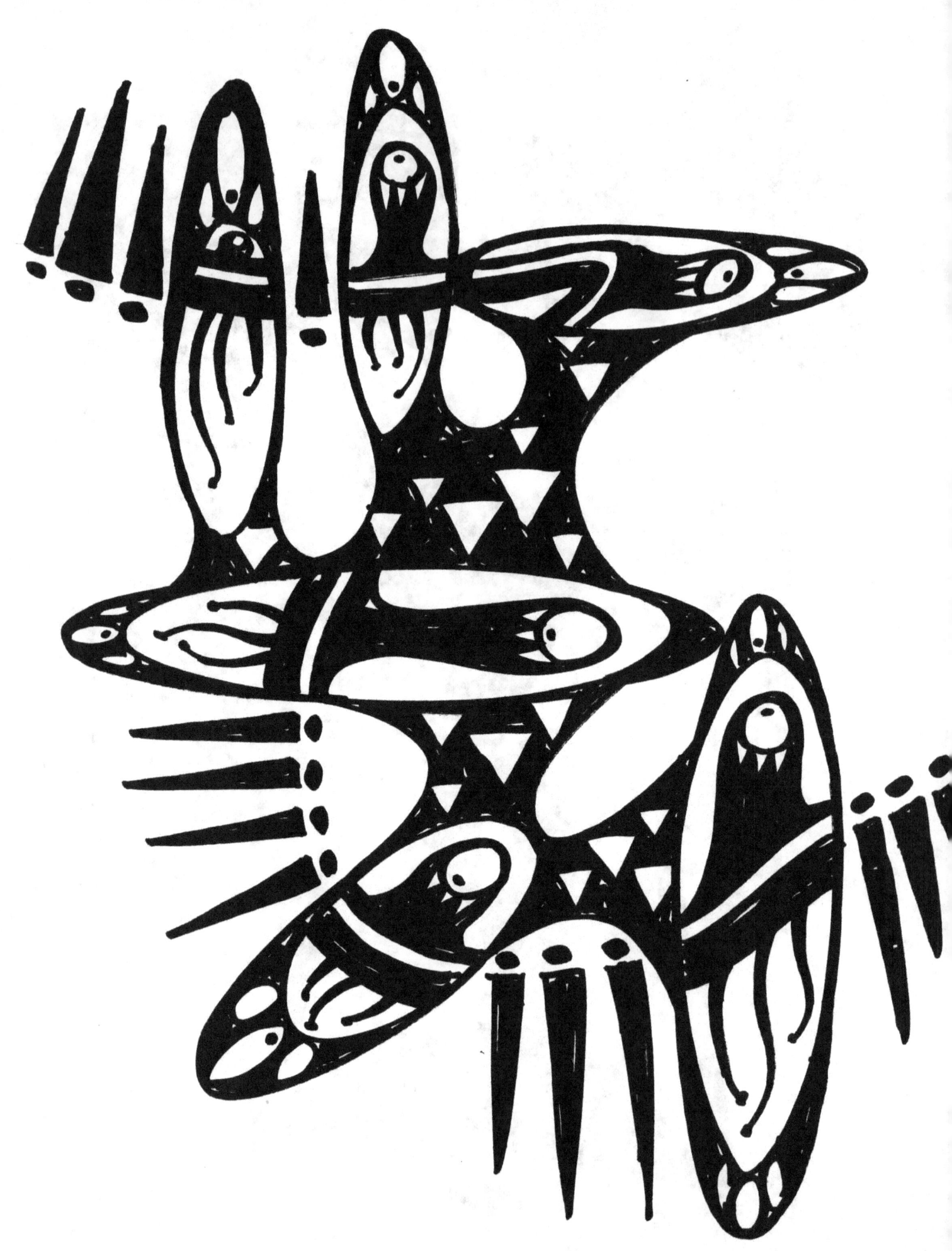

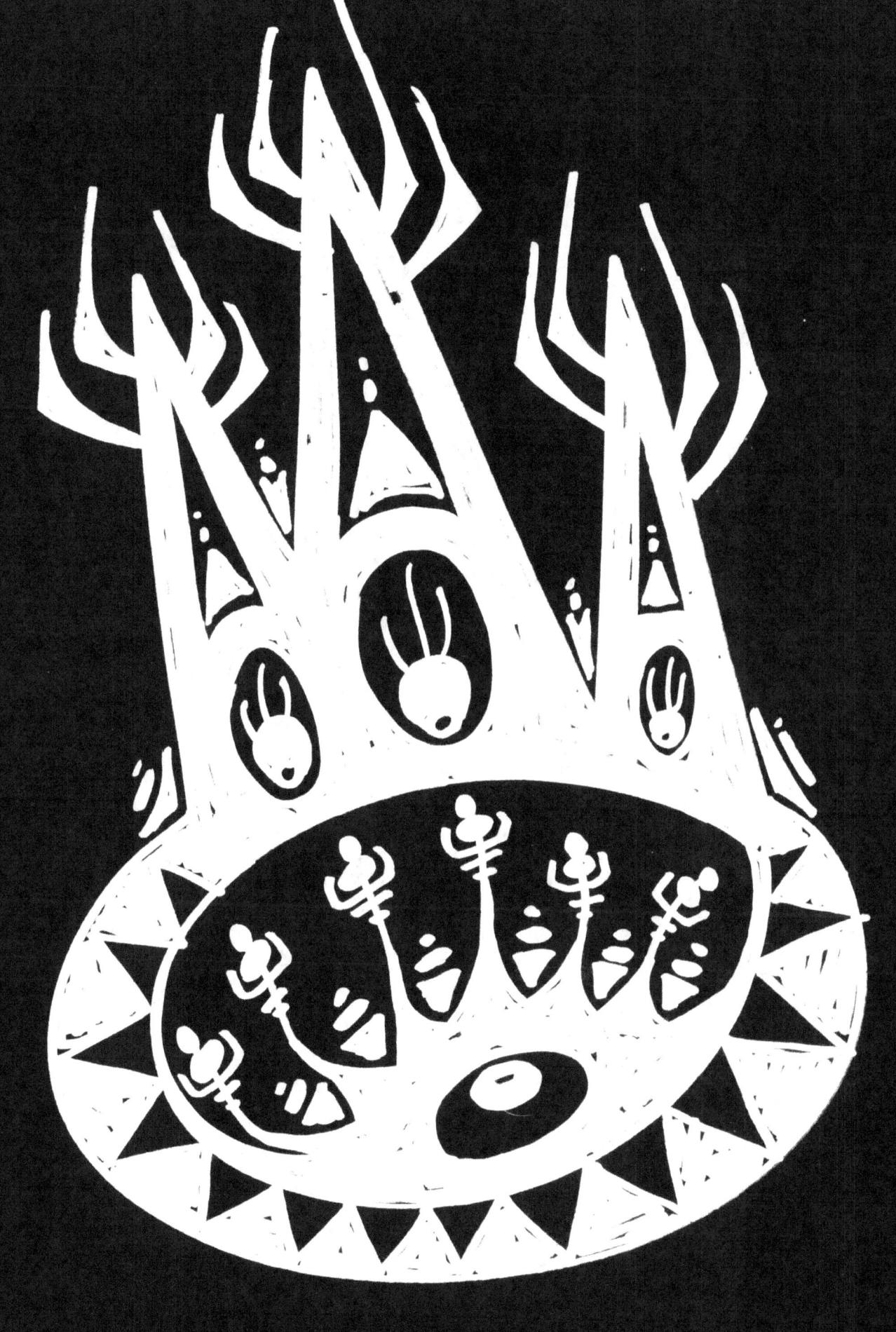

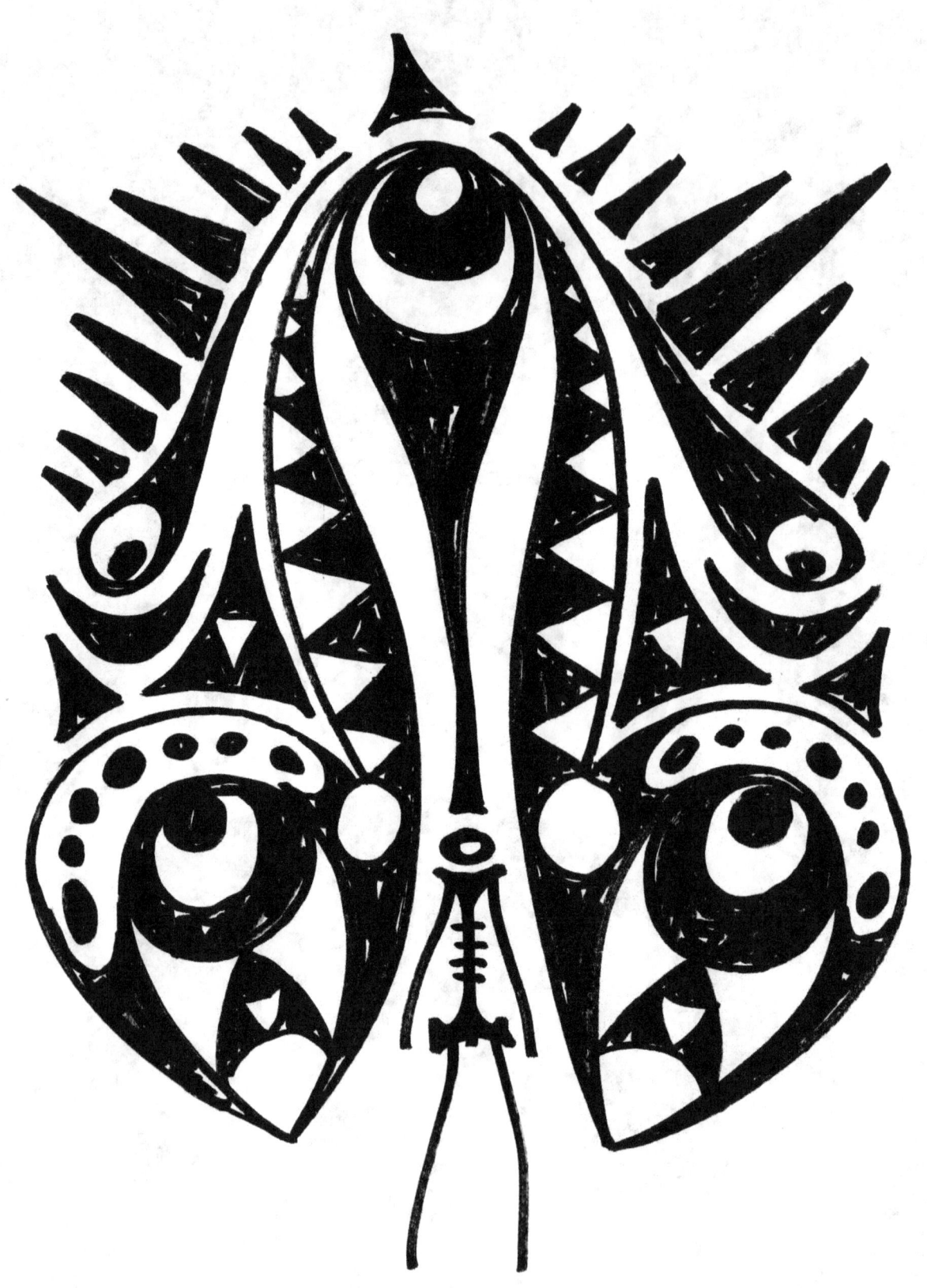

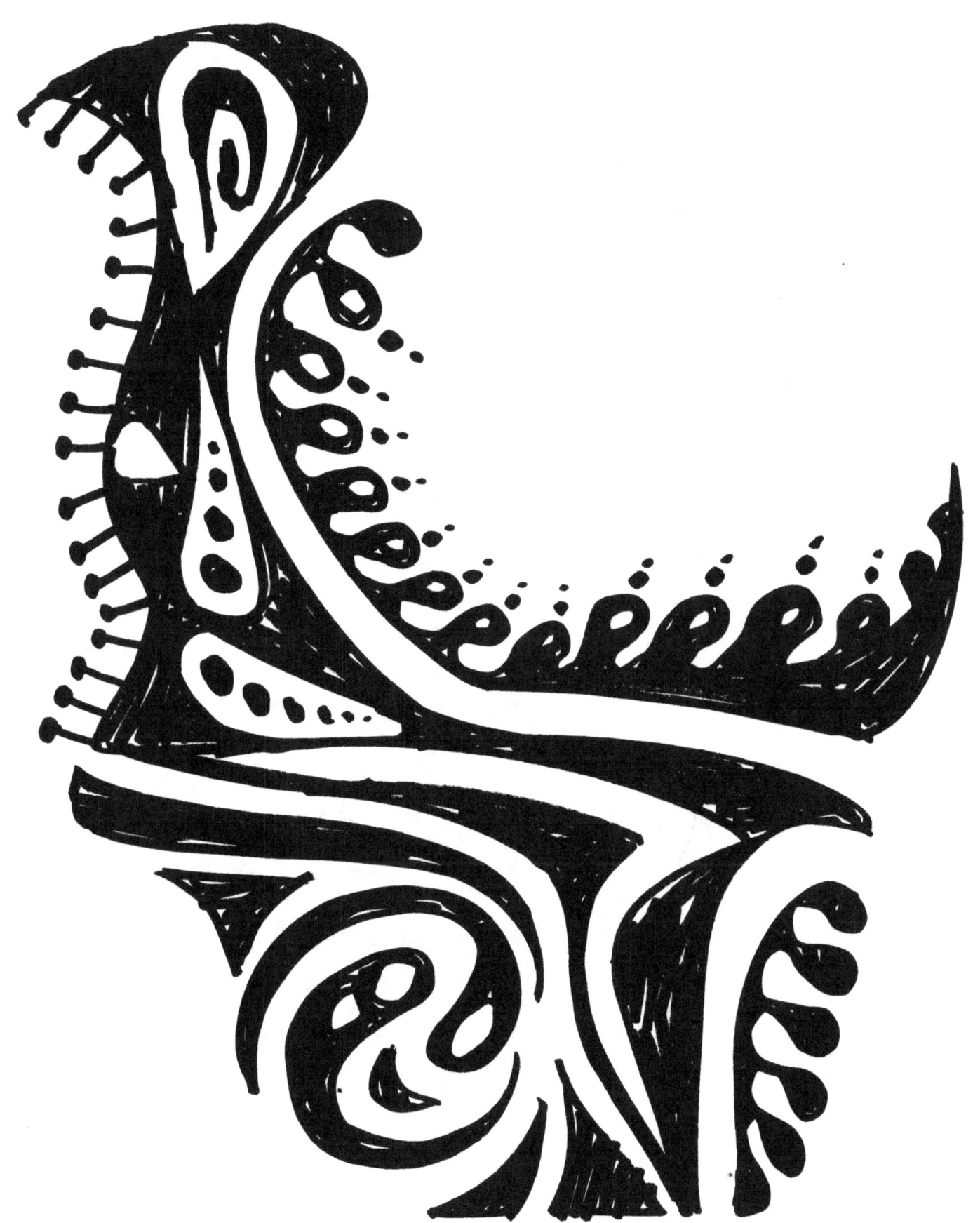

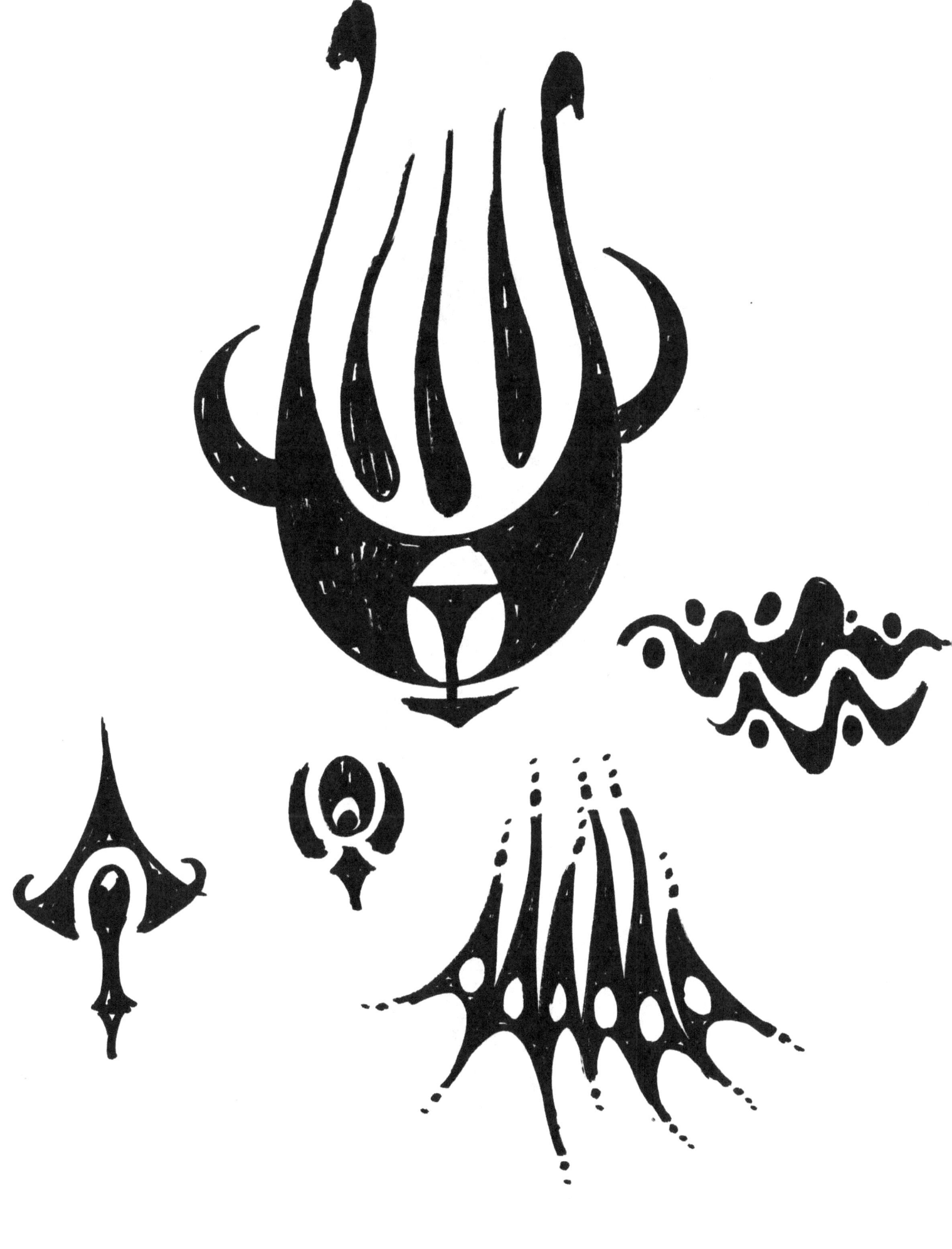

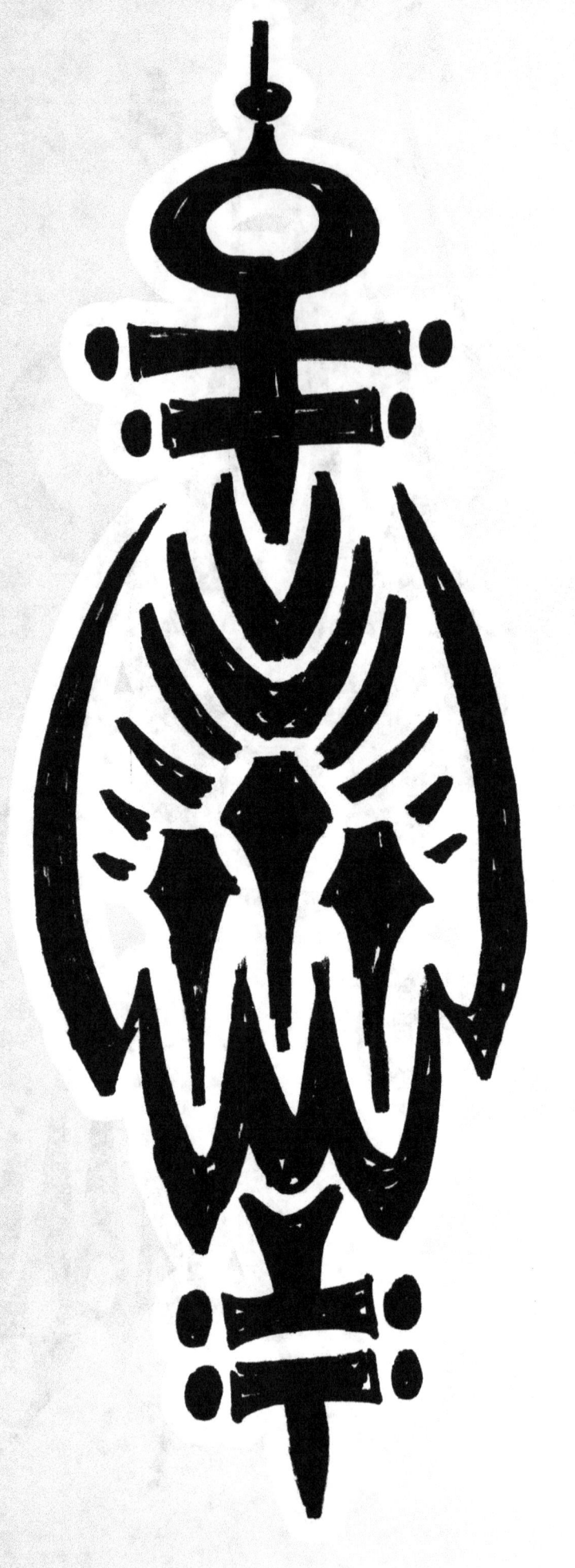

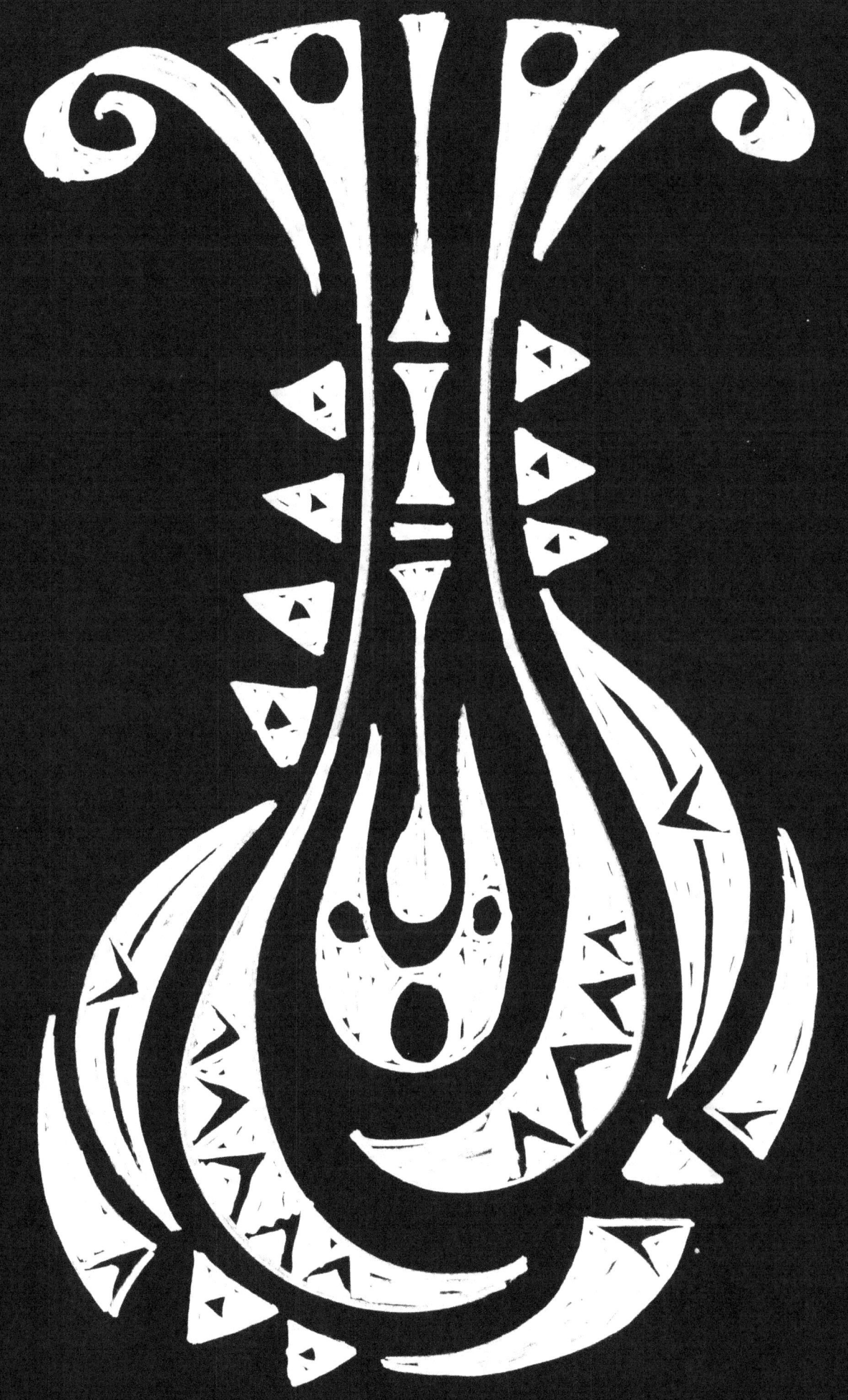

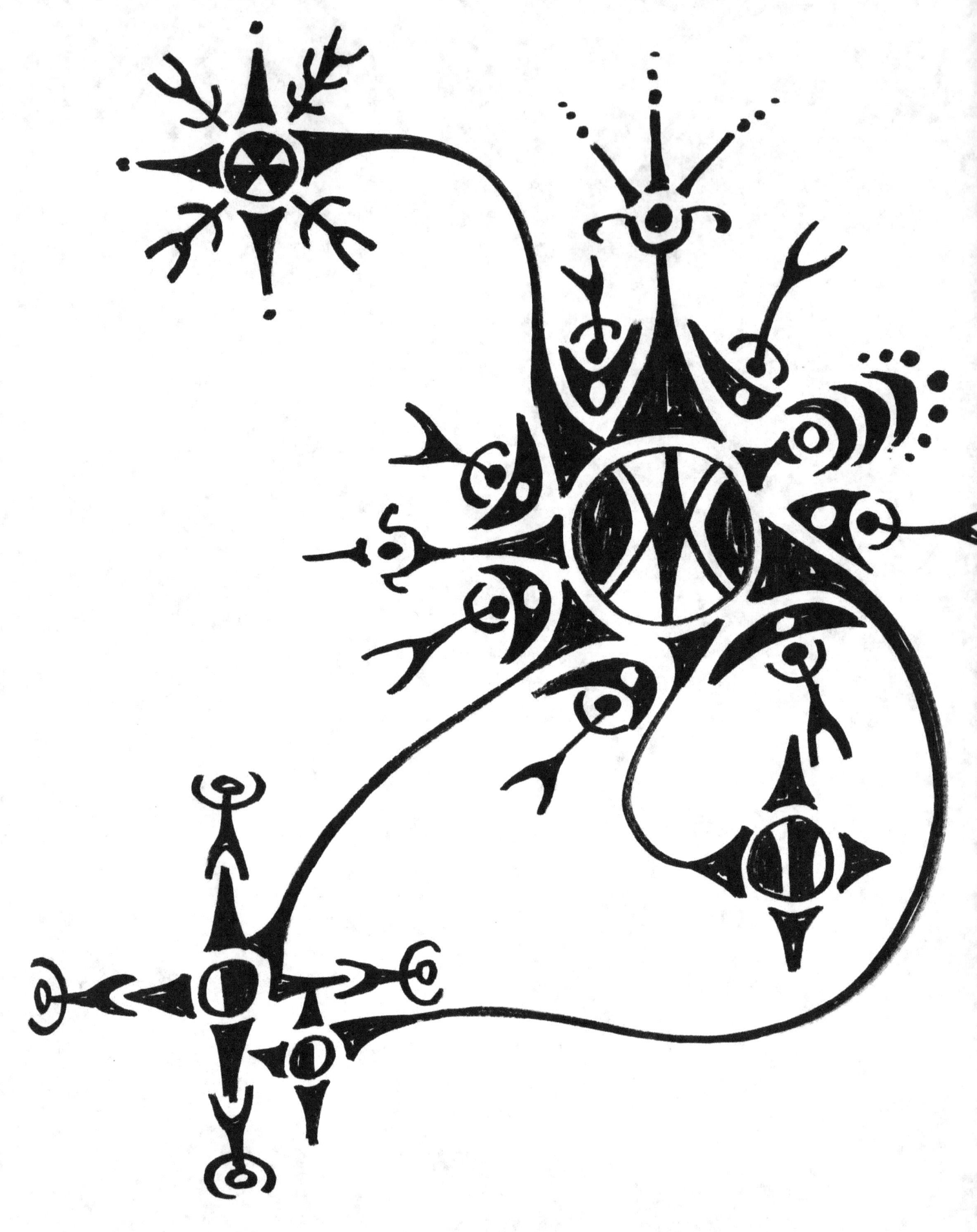

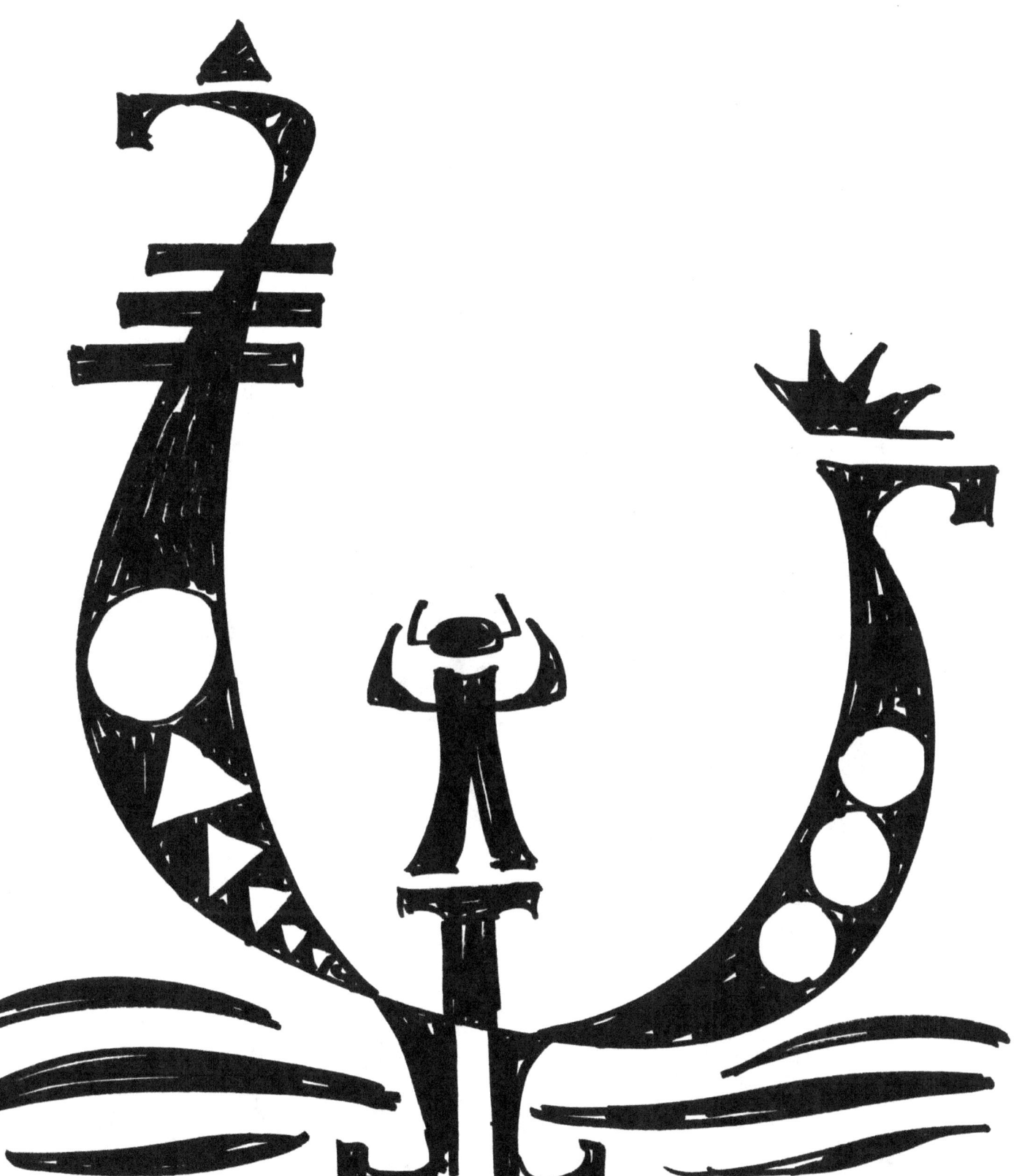

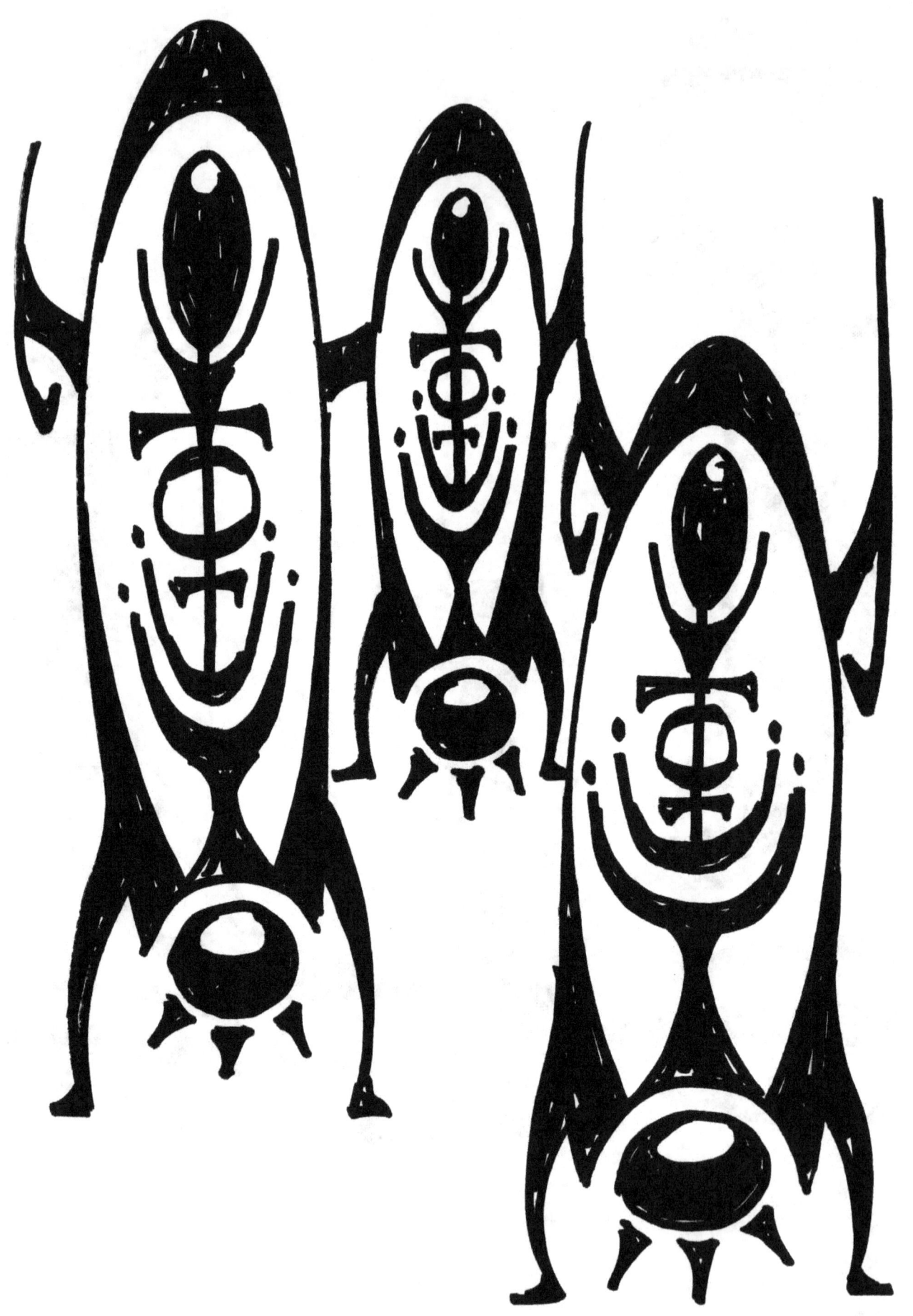

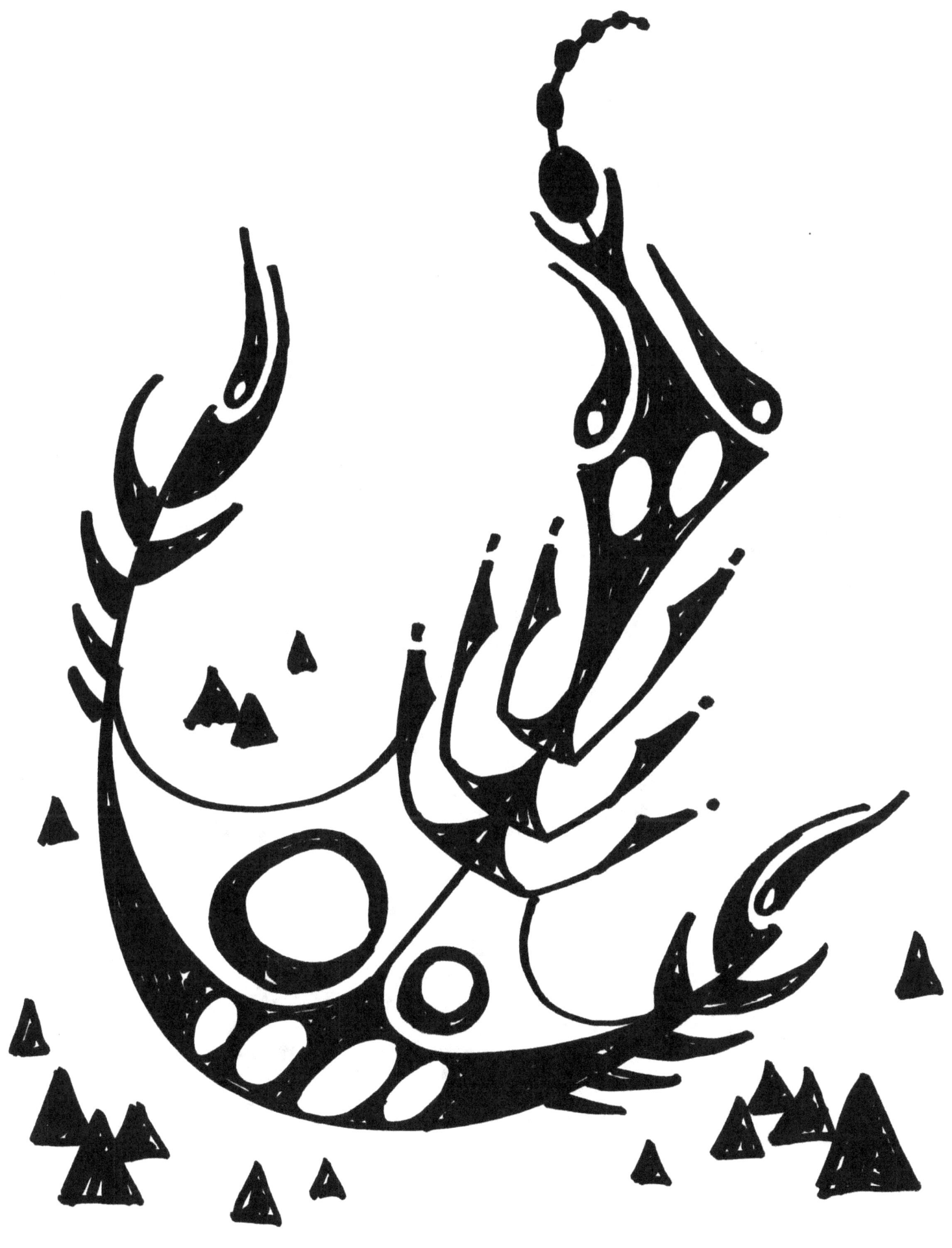

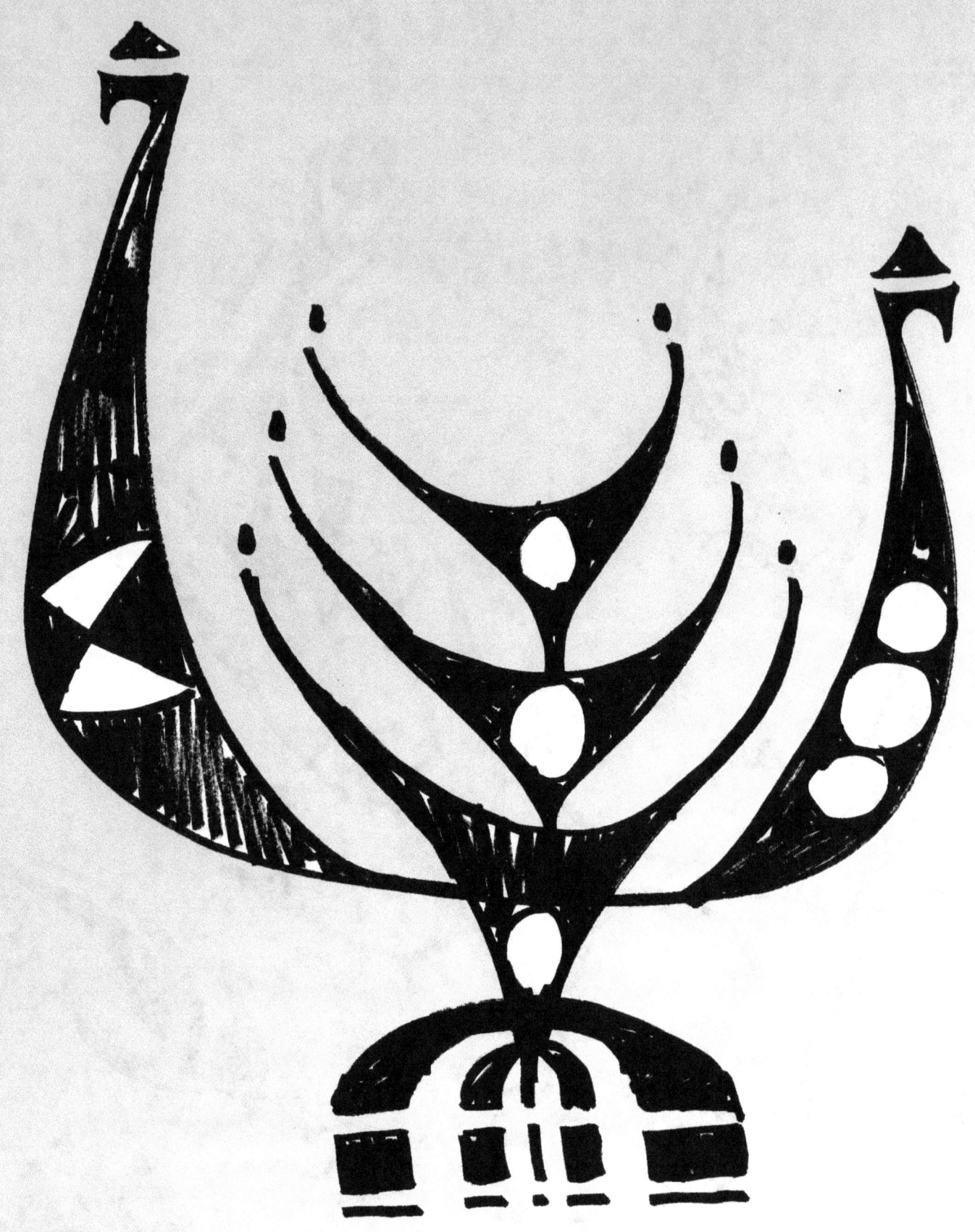

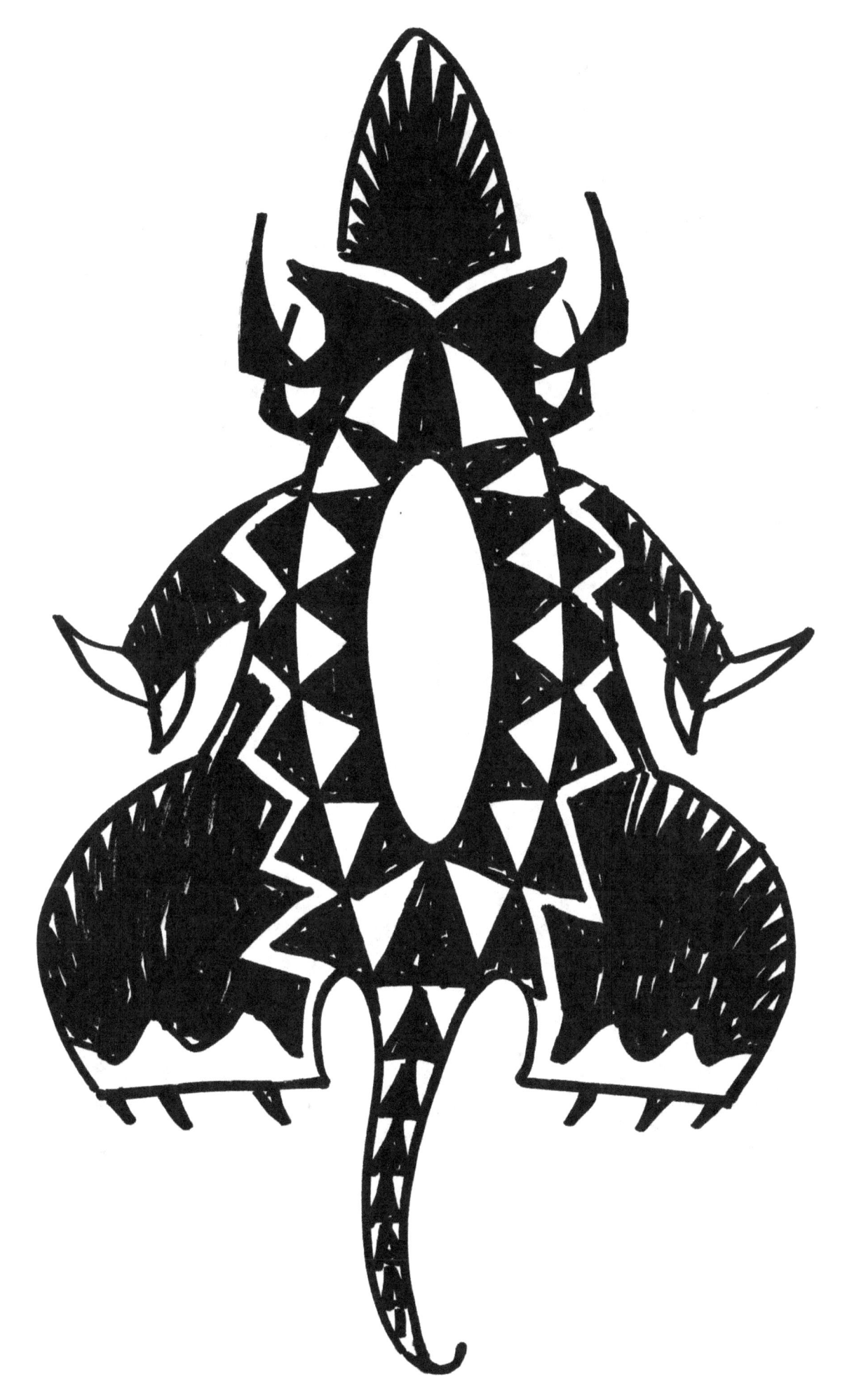

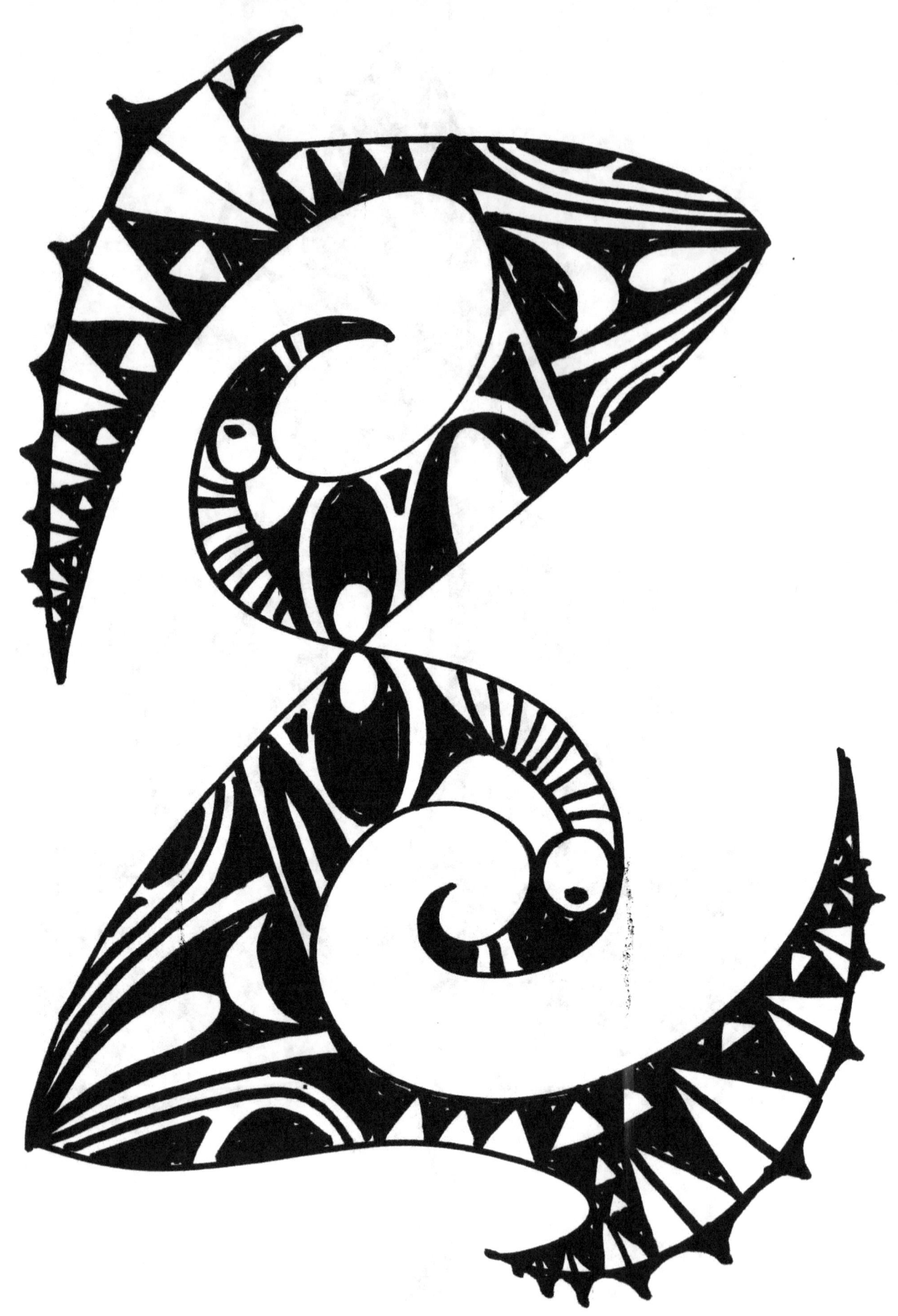

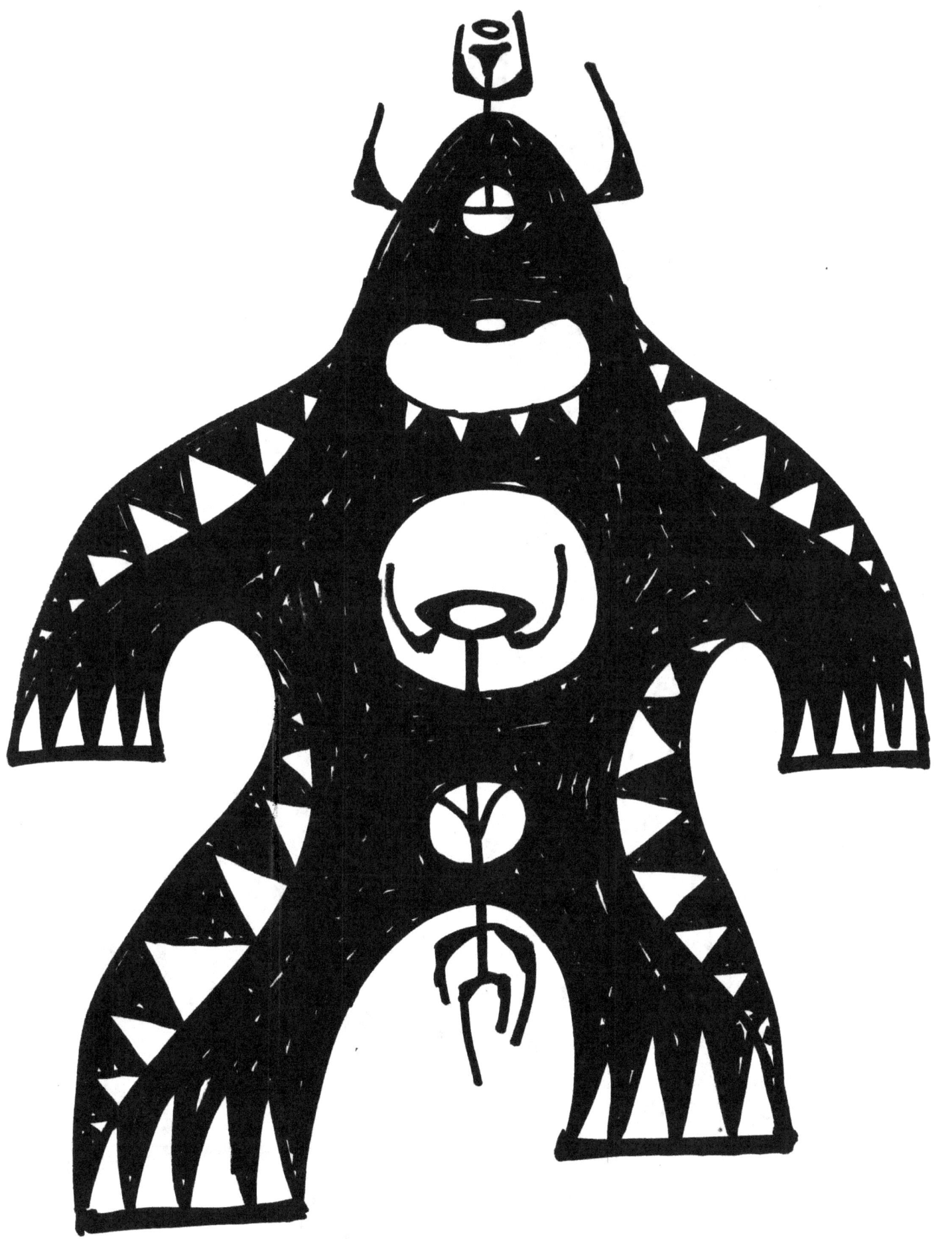

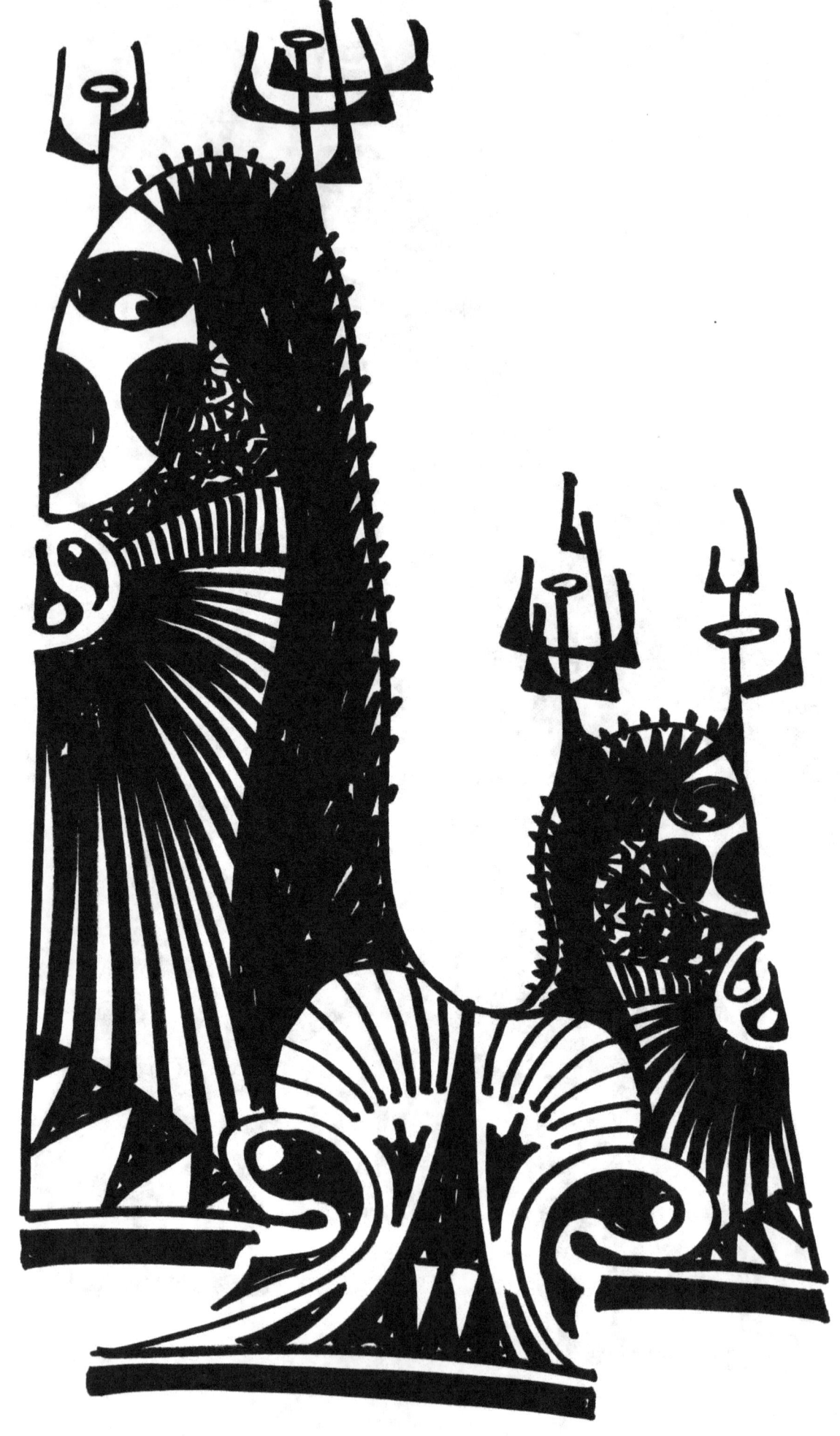

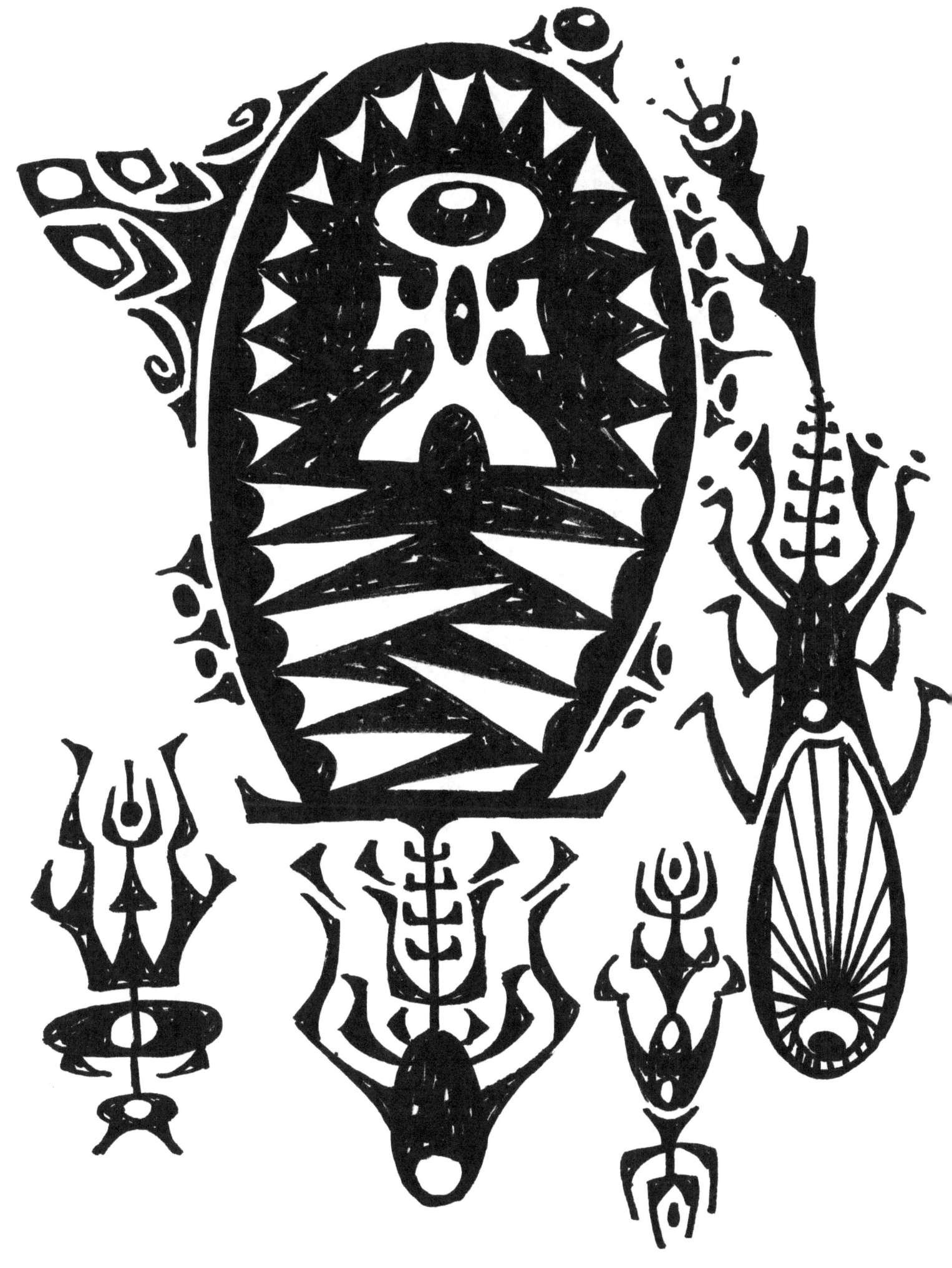

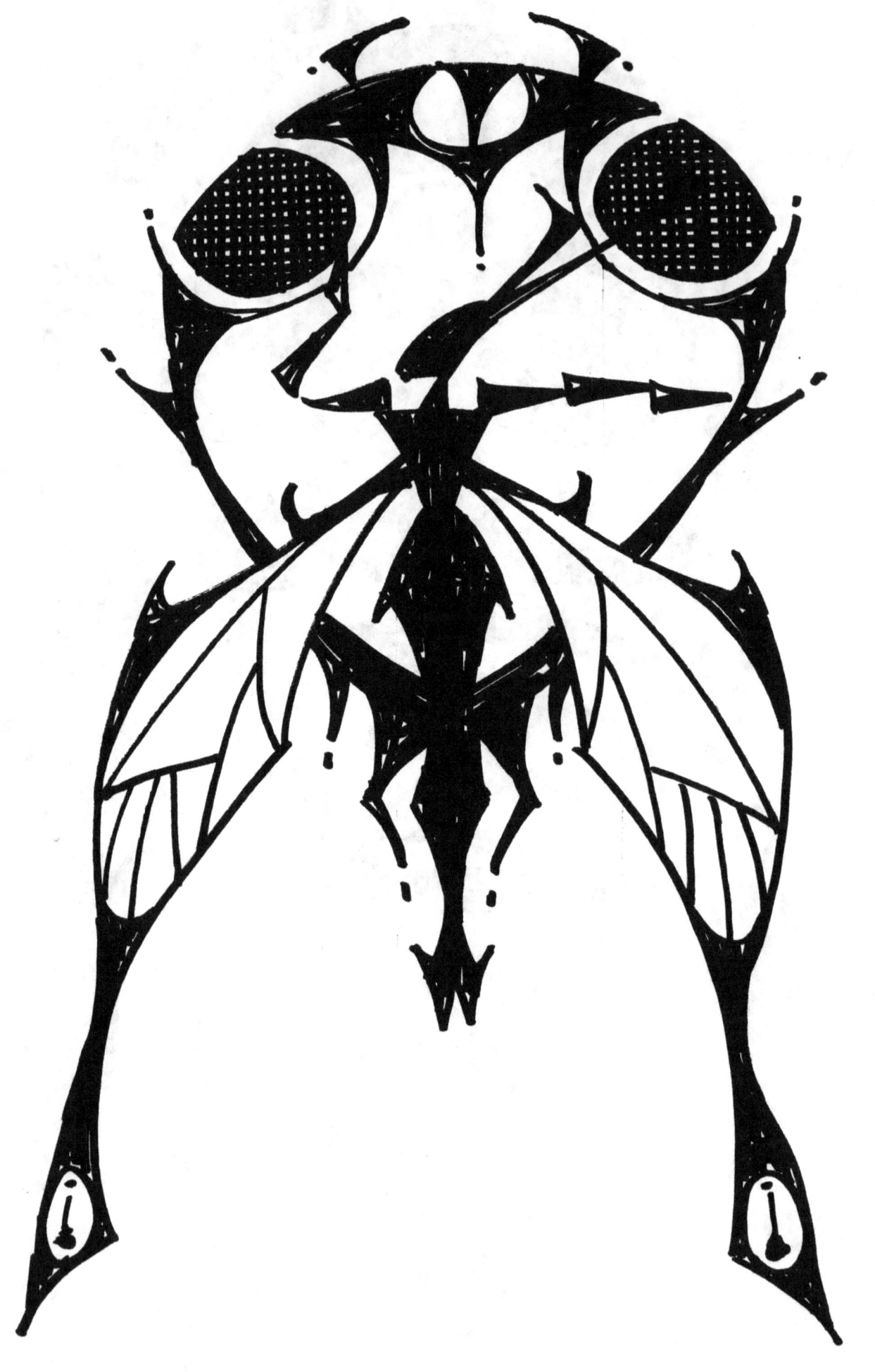

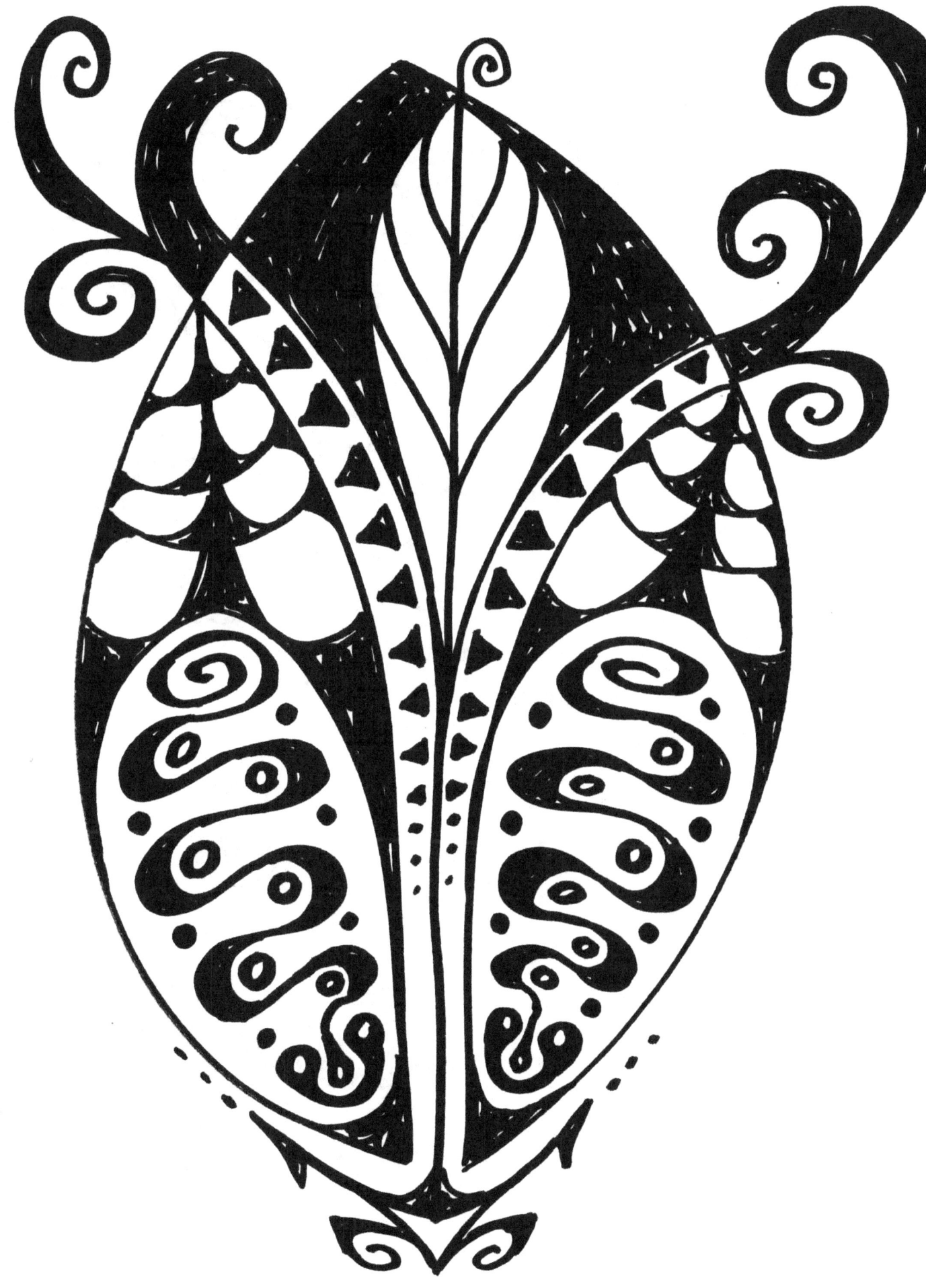

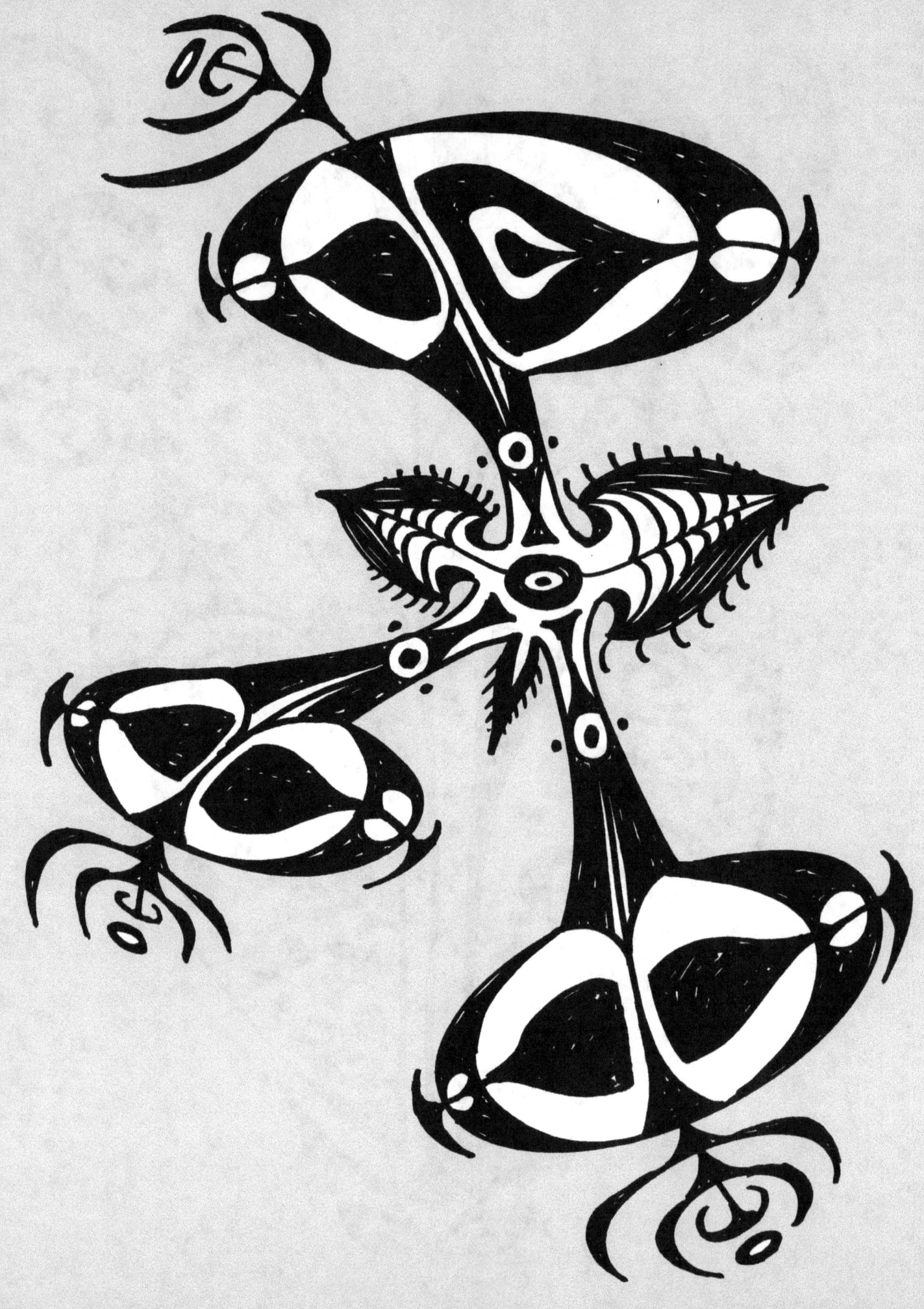

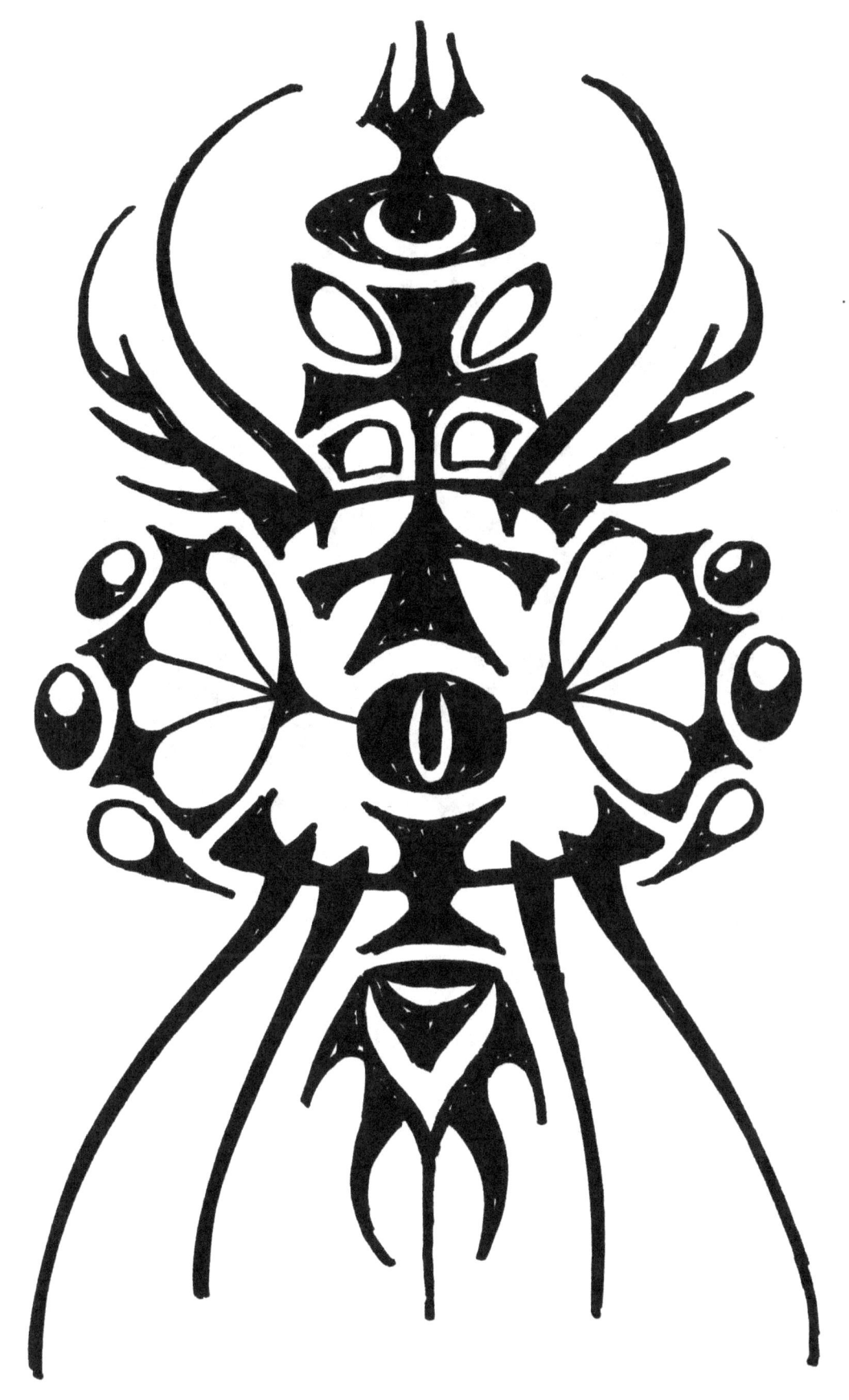

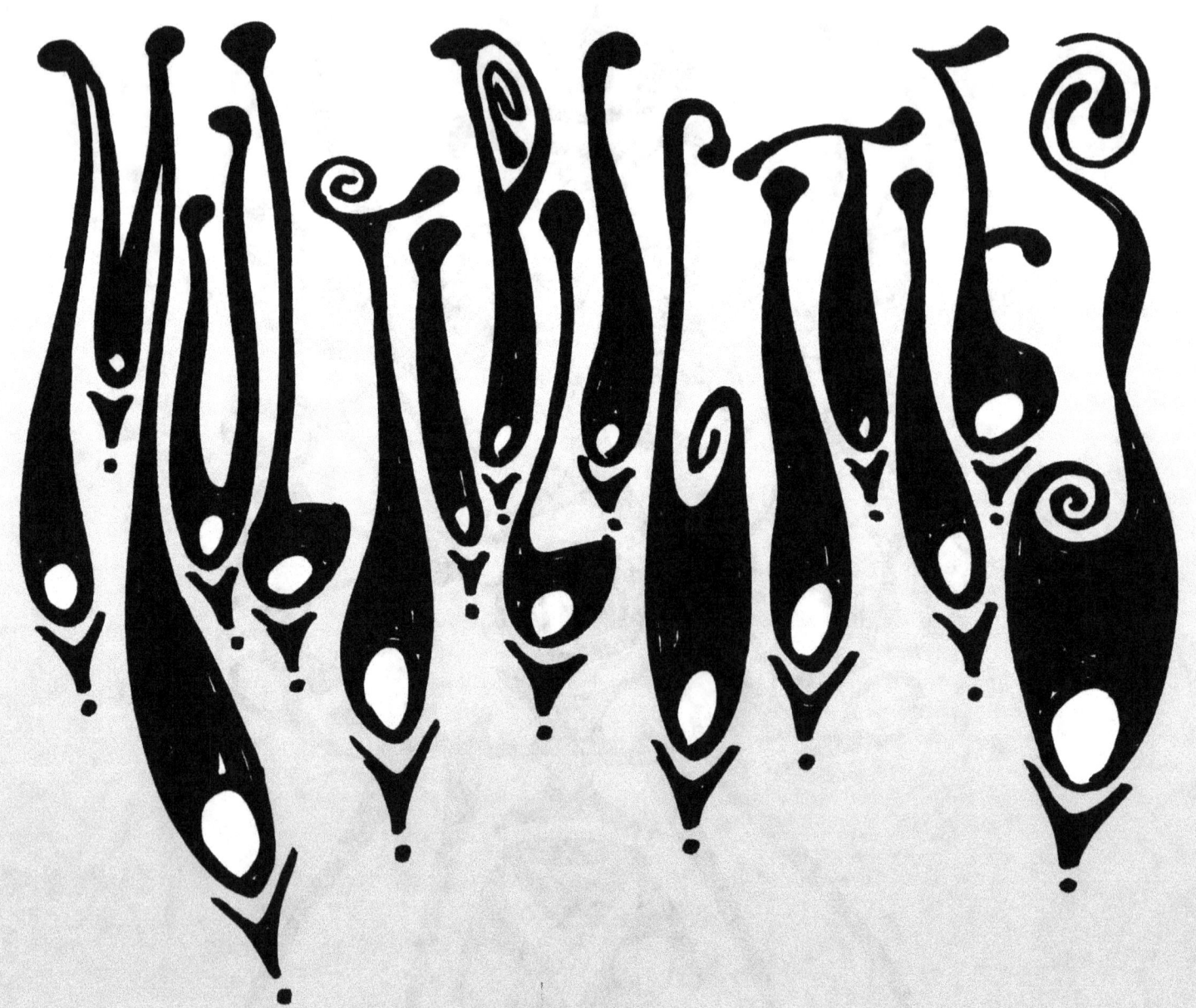

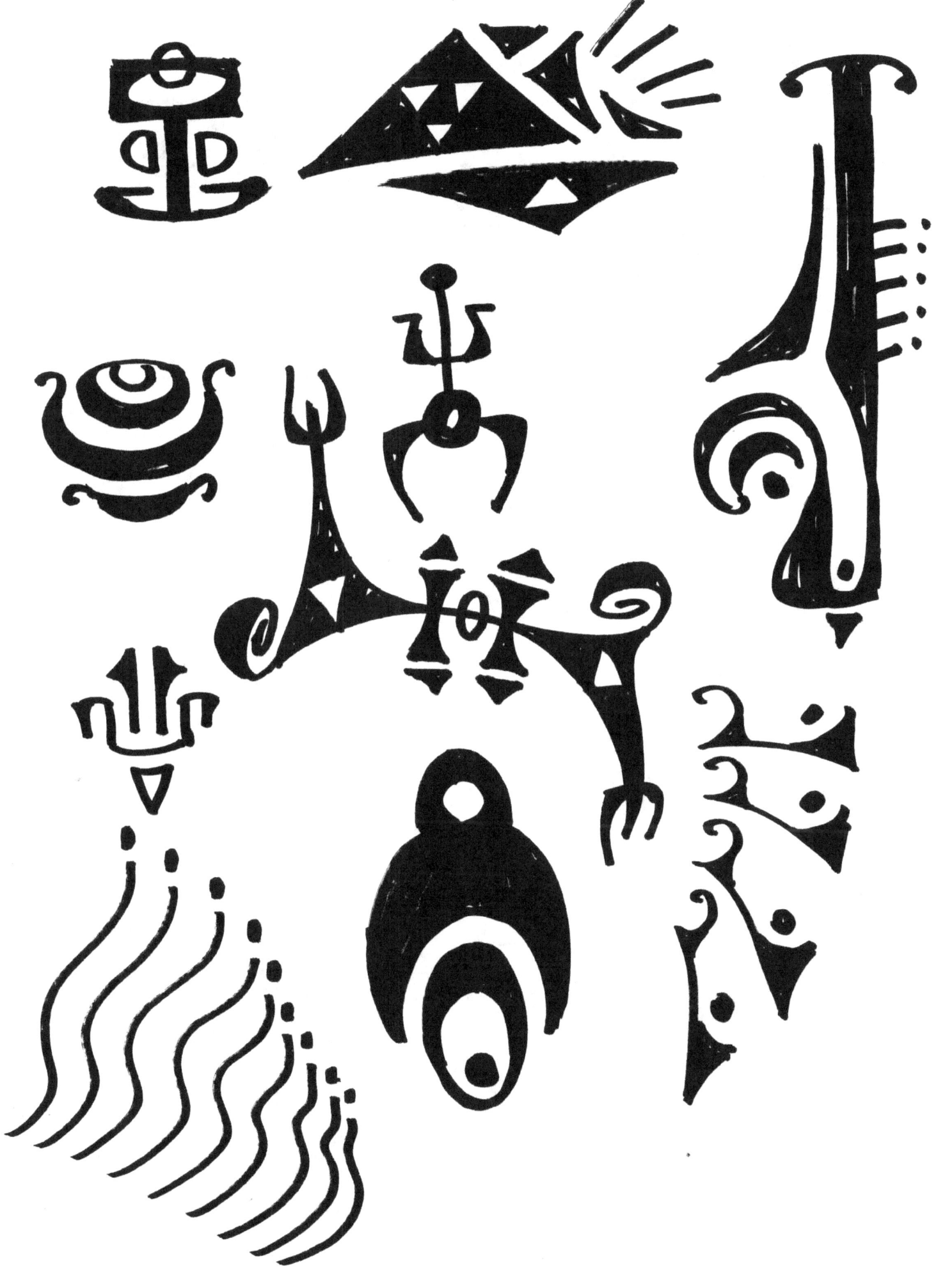

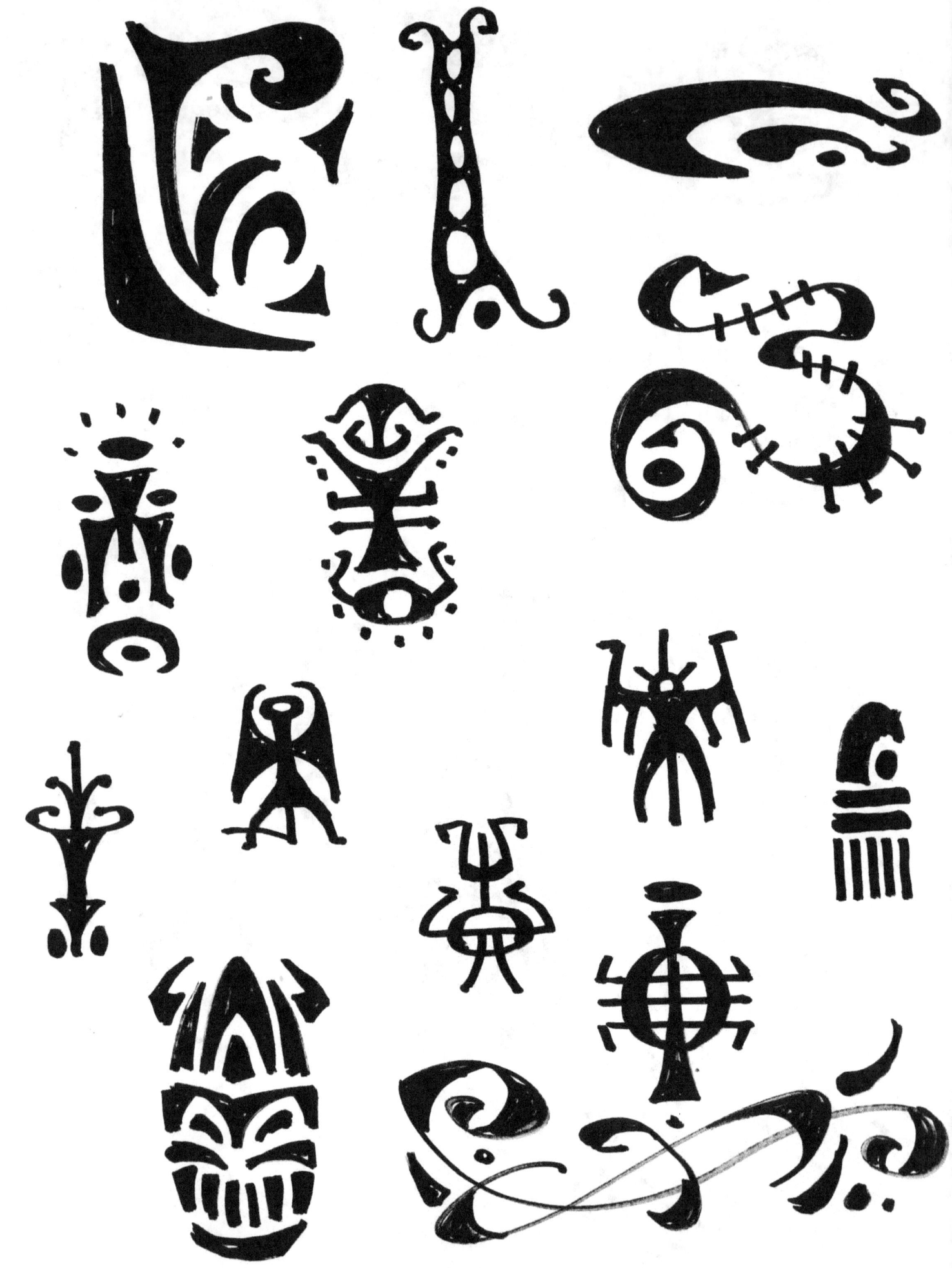

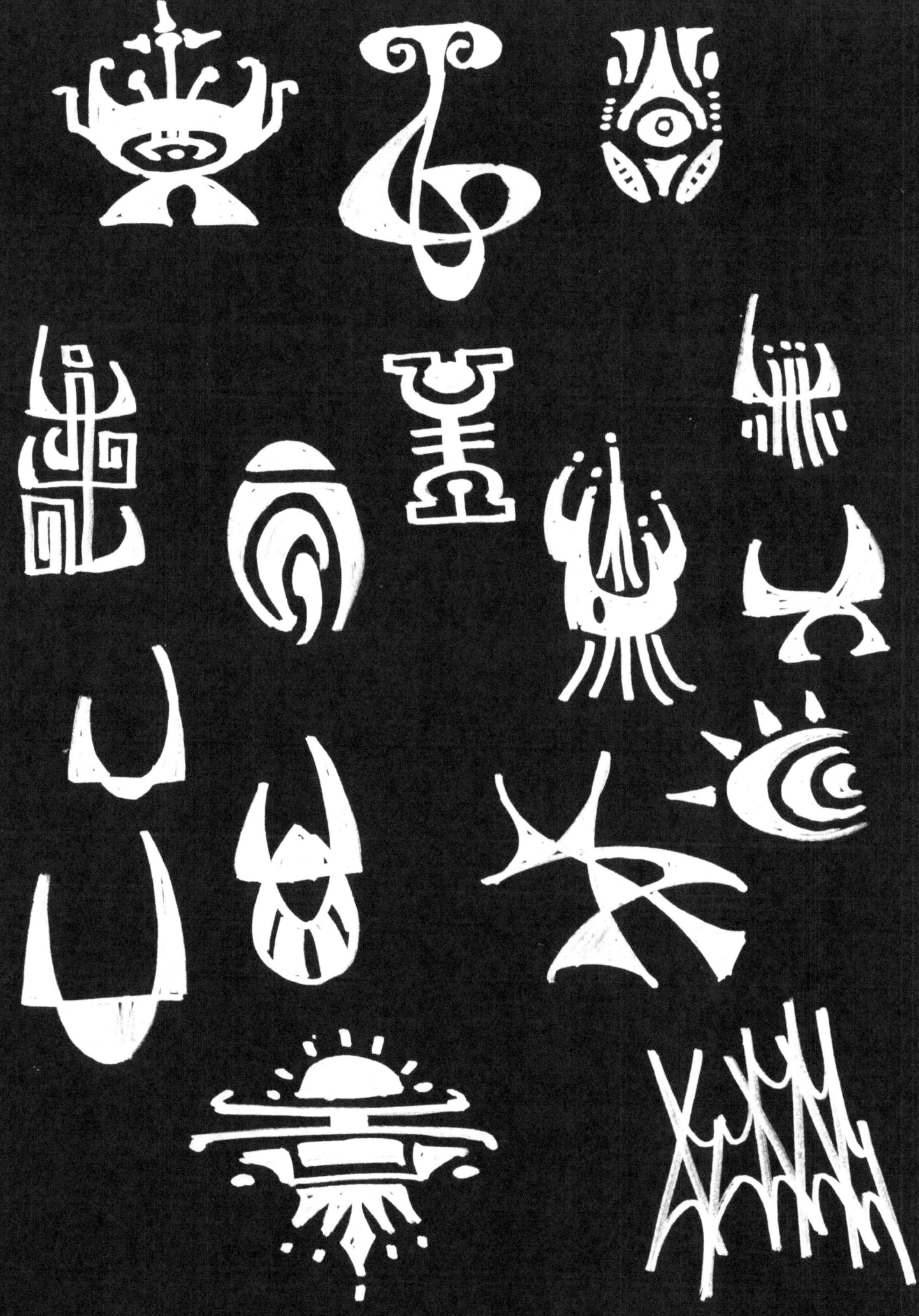

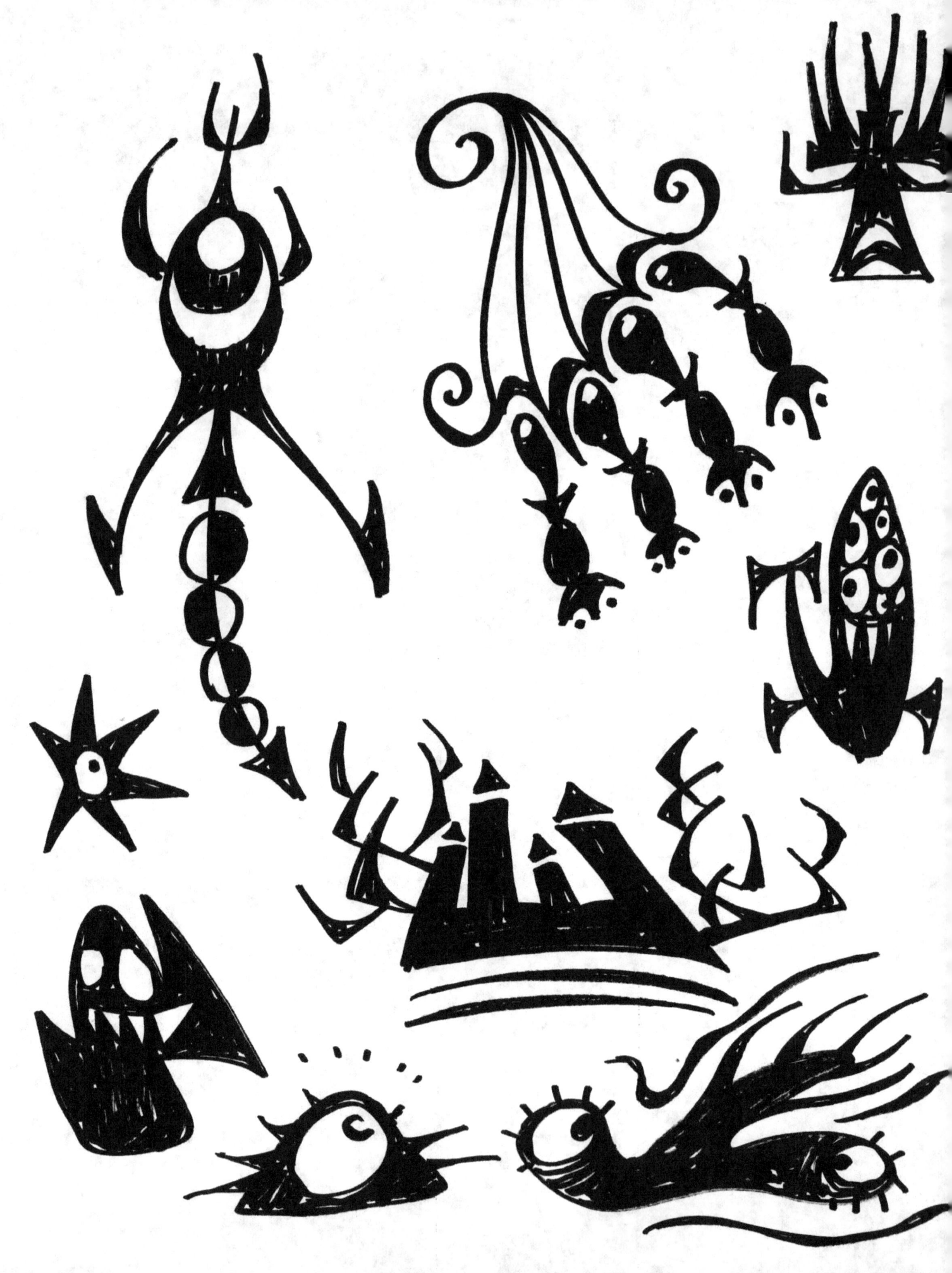

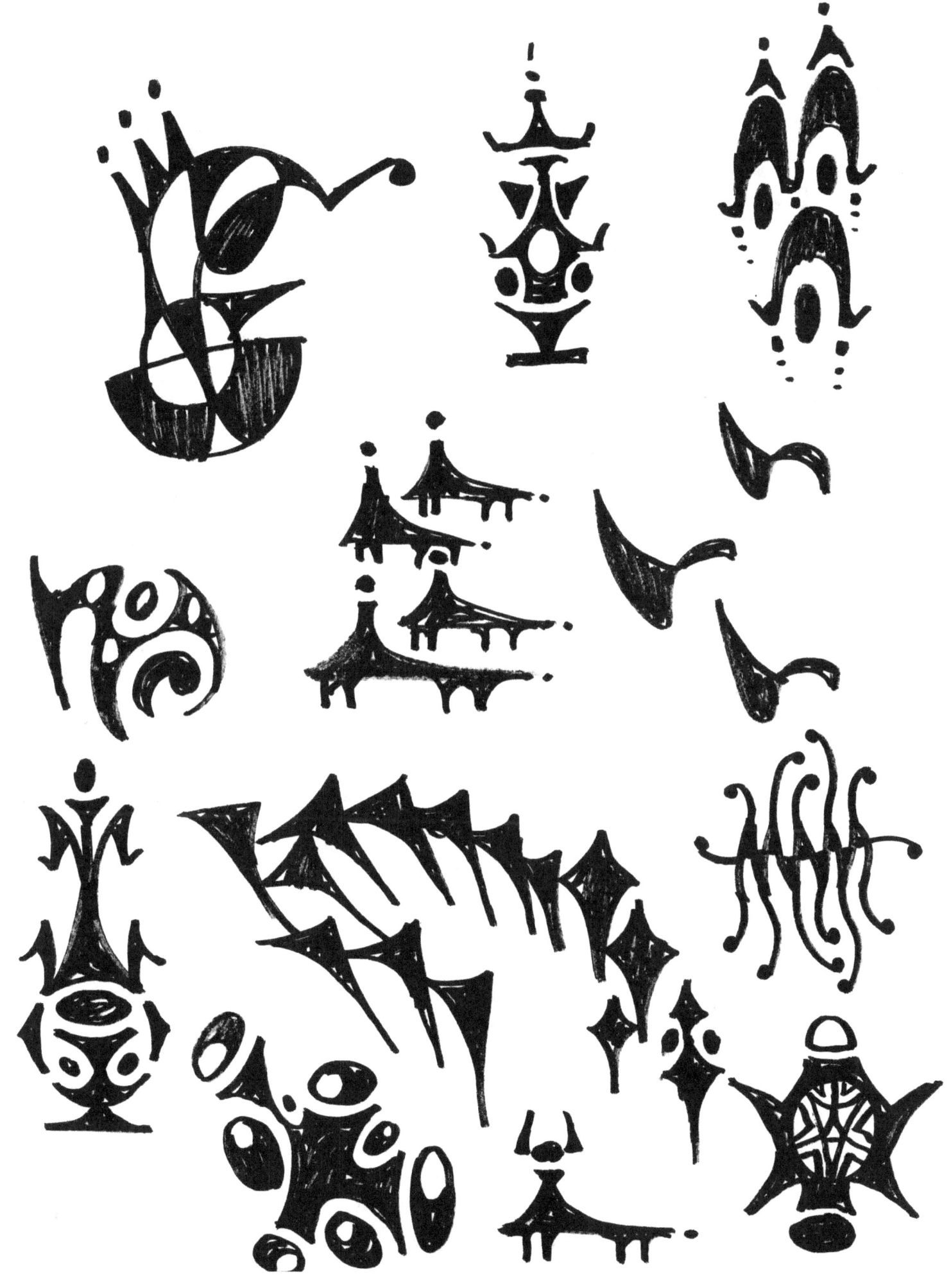

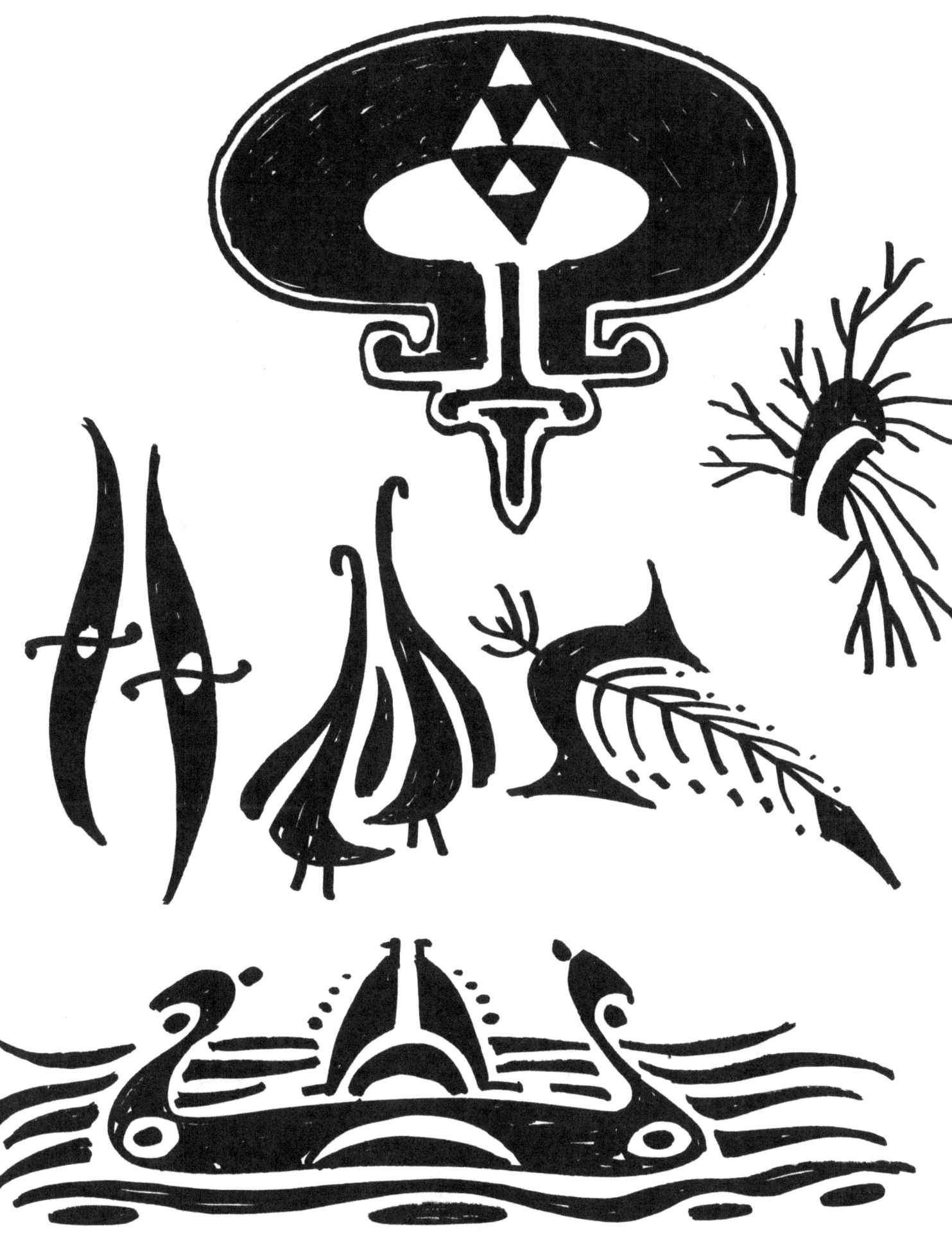

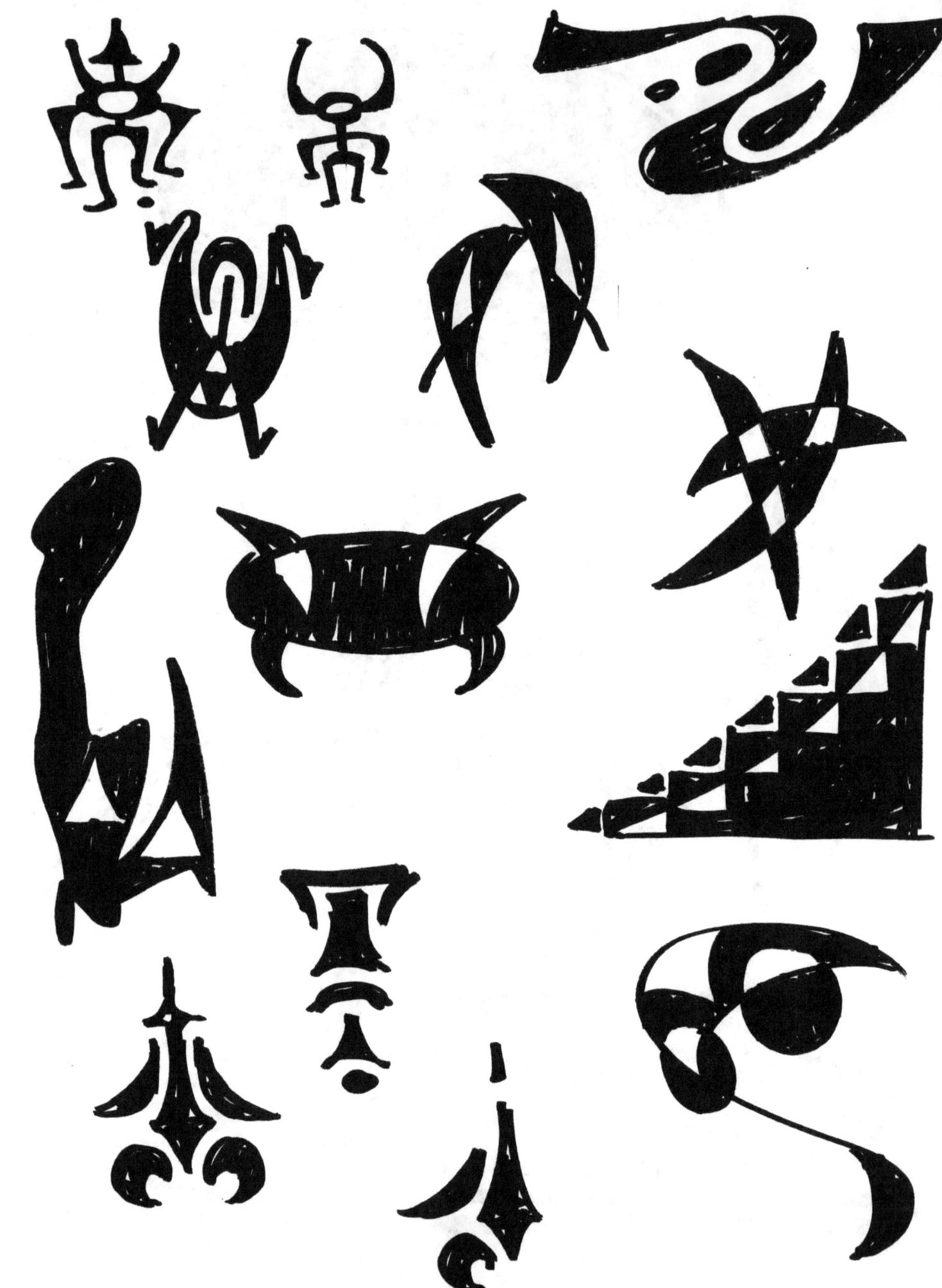

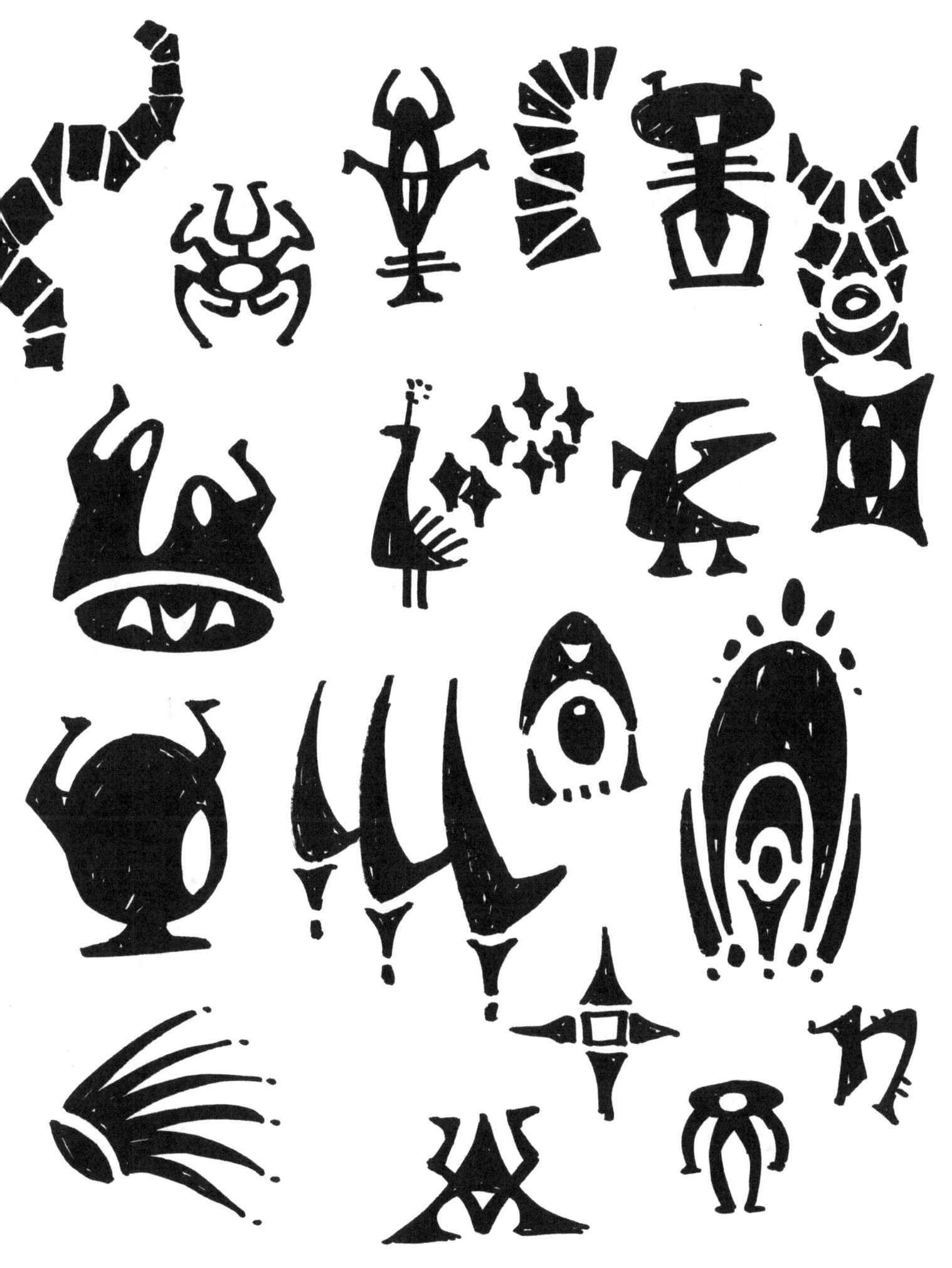

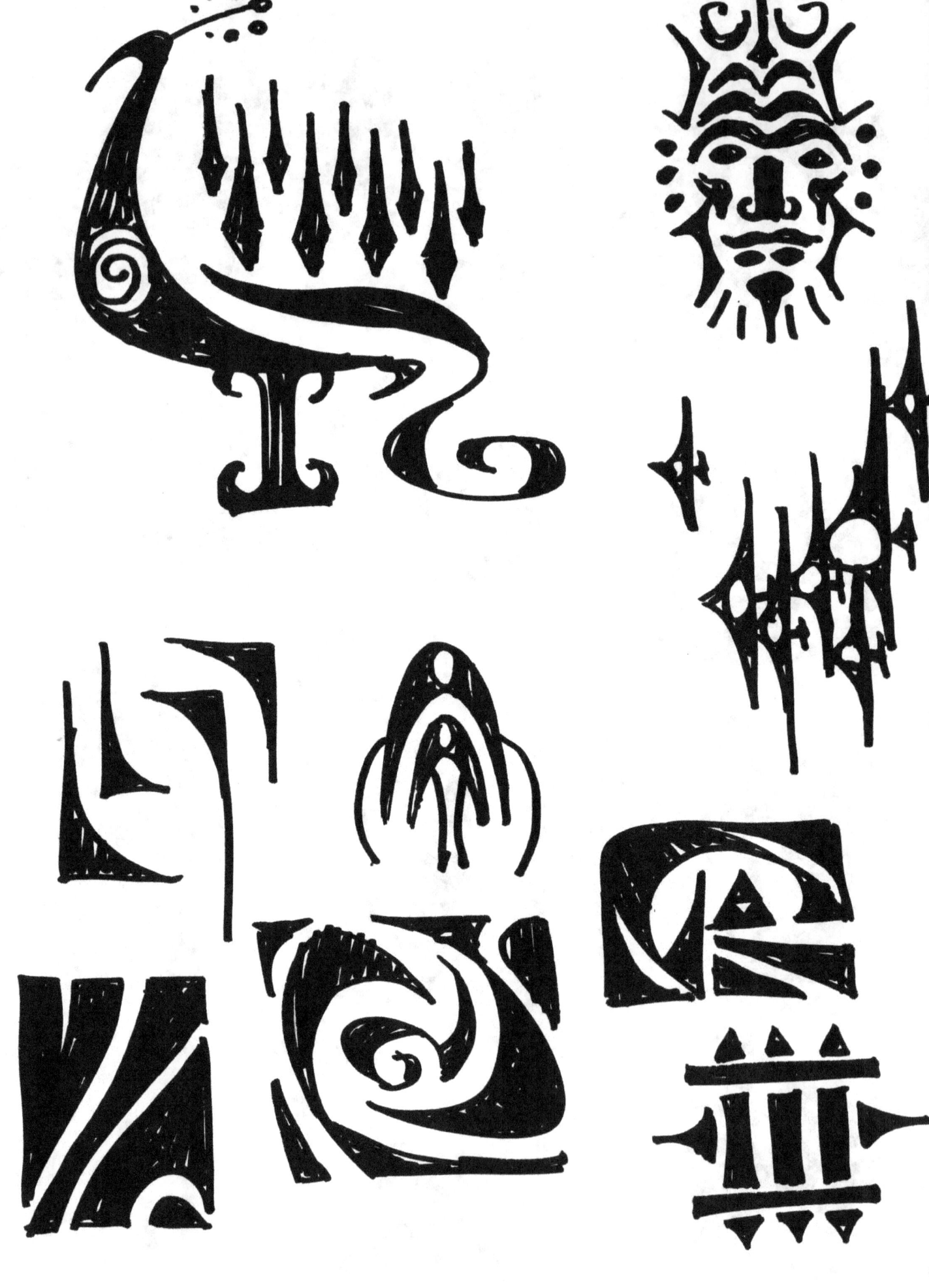

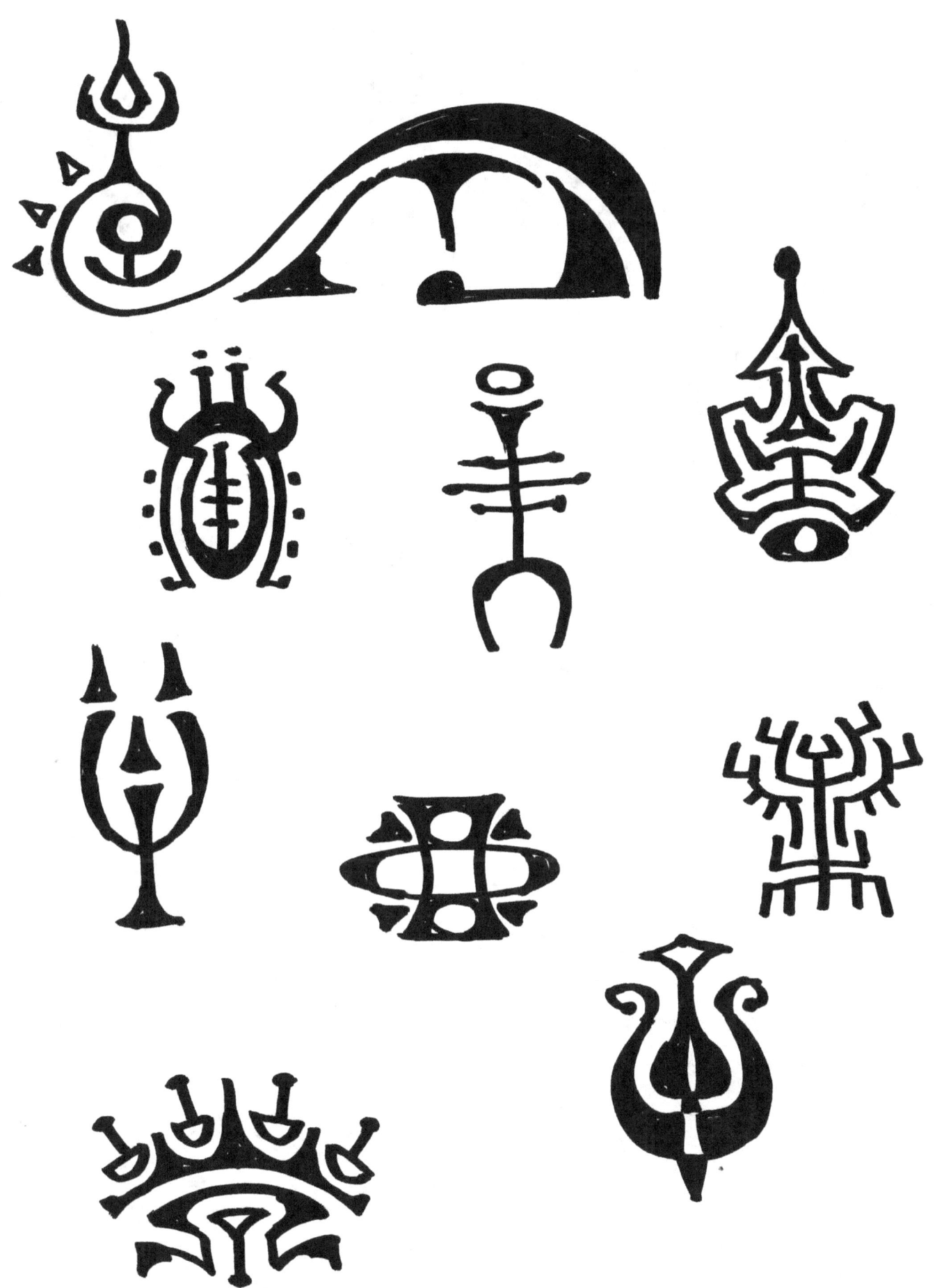

www.ingramcontent.com/pod-product-compliance
Lightning Source LLC
Chambersburg PA
CBHW081735170526
45167CB00009B/3828